CLASSIC PAINTS
AND
FAUX FINISHES

ANNIE SLOAN AND KATE GWYNN

CLASSIC PAINTS
AND
FAUX FINISHES

How to use natural materials
and authentic techniques
in today's decorating

Photography by
Geoff Dann

THE READER'S DIGEST ASSOCIATION, INC.
Pleasantville, New York/Montreal

CONTENTS

The Paint and Equipment Directory

The Color Directory

The House Painter's Techniques

A READER'S DIGEST BOOK

The credits and acknowledgments that appear on page 160 are
hereby made a part of this copyright page

Copyright © 1993 Collins & Brown Limited
All rights reserved. Unauthorized reproduction, in any manner, is prohibited

Library of Congress Cataloging in Publication Data

Sloan, Annie.
  Classic paints and faux finishes: how to use natural materials and
authentic techniques in today's decorating / Annie Sloan and Kate Gwynn.
      p.   cm.
  Includes index.
  ISBN 0-89577-523-9
  1. Painting—Technique.   2. Decoration and ornament.   3. Paint.
  I. Gwynn, Kate.   II. Title.
TT385.S555   1993
745.7—dc20   93-5027

Reader's Digest and the Pegasus logo are registered trademarks
of The Reader's Digest Association, Inc.
Printed and bound in Italy by New Interlitho SpA, Milan

The Furniture Painter's Techniques

The Artist's Techniques

The Restorer's Techniques

Conceived, edited, and designed by Collins & Brown Limited

Editors: Linda Doeser and Colin Ziegler
Art Director: Roger Bristow
Designer: Steven Wooster
Photography: Geoff Dann

Introduction

WE HAVE WRITTEN this book because of the growing interest in natural pigments and materials, and the newly revitalized techniques which comprise today's most popular trend in home decorating. This interest began about 15 years ago when some specialty decorative oil glazes and paint finishes were reintroduced to the marketplace and there was a revival of interest in traditional techniques such as sponging, ragging, and faux finishes, first used in Europe as early as the 17th century.

Time, too, has proved that paints and other finishes made from ingredients and pigments found in nature create softer, subtler colors and give more pleasing effects than ordinary, mass-produced, plastic paints. Today, the vogue for classic paints has spread into more specialized fields – those of the artist, furniture maker, gilder, and restorer – all of whom have seen these authentic glazes and other finishes as a way of expanding their own decorative ideas. These artists and craftspeople have gone on to explore and reintroduce other classic skills and materials. The arts of découpage, lacquer, and even fresco have taken on a new lease of life, and the use of glue size, old varnishes, and waxes has been renewed. Ancient decorating manuals have been consulted, conversations with those who practice traditional crafts have been written down, and surviving examples of classic techniques have been preserved and now serve as reference.

This delving into the past is not simply the result of a wave of nostalgia. It is a reaction to the blandness and uniformity of modern paints. Although easy to use, modern paints tend to have similar textures as they are plastic paints, that is, based on polymers, vinyl acetates, and acrylics. They are available in a bewildering array of colors, yet the pigments used to color them are so standardized and ground so finely that these colors tend to be uniform and lack individuality.

Classic paints and finishes, on the other hand, offer a refreshing variation in texture – from the flat/mat, slightly uneven quality of limewash, size paints, and fresco, to the gloss of shellacs and resin varnishes. The pigments used to color these paints are often crudely ground and unevenly dispersed in the paint mixture, so that when the paint is applied, the color comes through more strongly in some areas than in others, creating a splendidly unique and hand-crafted surface.

Traditional paints have the added attraction of being environmentally friendly. Unlike modern plastic paints, they do not rely on the petro-chemical industry for their manufacture. Most of their ingredients come from plants, or other natural products such as earth pigments, and they tend to work in harmony with the environment. Authentic paints such as limewash, for example, are absorbed into the surface on which they are applied and allow walls to "breathe" as, unlike with modern, plastic paints, moisture is not trapped by a film of plastic.

Our first chapter, *The Paint and Equipment Directory*, introduces the raw materials used to make paints, the different types of paints and other

A simple design can be greatly enhanced by using a subtle variety of colors to add contrast and tone (opposite). Annie Sloan first drew the design with a soft lead pencil on a surface rubbed with earth colored pigments and an off-white paint. She then highlighted certain areas with a white paint (below).

Annie Sloan used her fingertips to apply the finishing touches (above). Further variations in shade can be achieved by removing the pigment in places with an eraser.

finishes that there are, and the equipment needed for their application. There is today, a tremendous range of paints available, some of which can be found in your standard paint or hardware store, others from specialty art stores and supply companies which specialize in authentic paints, and a few which have to be made up from their basic ingredients. The way in which paint is applied to the surface is of course integral to the finished look and, depending on the task at hand, there are specific materials and tools for preparing the surface and for applying the paint or finish. For the first time, our book tells you what paints are available and how to obtain and use them.

Most people's first reaction to paint is based on its color and *The Color Directory* includes historical and practical information on the different pigments available. It looks at the glorious array of colors and types of paint traditionally found in different parts of the world, and gives advice on how different colors should be mixed to produce the desired result.

The techniques for both making and using classic paints and other finishes have then been divided into four broad categories covered in the remaining sections of the book: *The House Painter's Techniques, The Furniture Painter's Techniques, The Artist's Techniques,* and *The Restorer's Techniques.* For each of these, the manufacture and application of paint and other finishes has, in the past, existed at two different levels. At a basic level, the peasant or farmer would himself use whatever materials were locally available to protect and decorate his home. At a more sophisticated level, the rich commissioned highly-skilled artists and decorators, using a far greater range of materials, to do the task for them. The book covers these techniques, both primitive and sophisticated, each creating a unique paint effect.

In the case of house painting, peasants and farmers traditionally coated their walls with limewash, or other simple paints based on milk or glue size. The result varied from a delicate and even finish to a vibrant, uneven coat, depending on the application. These paints age well, are esthetically pleasing and suit conservationists and environmentalists.

At a more advanced level, professional artists and decorators would grind chunks of dried pigment in a pestle and mortar or mechanical grinding mill and then, like a medieval alchemist, concoct their paints using a wide range of different materials. The latter included resins (from trees), animal glue, chalk, egg, flour, milk, and a whole variety of oils, like walnut, poppy, and linseed oil. Each of these unique paint effects is considered in turn, from simple coatings, glazes and limewash, to casein and size paints.

Next we look at *The Furniture Painter's Techniques.* The high point of furniture decoration was in the 18th century, when professional craftsmen used a whole range of techniques, such as gilding, lacquer, and découpage, to embellish furniture for the grand houses of the time. Many of the techniques originated in the East and arrived in the West via Italy and Flanders. They often involve using exotic materials like bronze powders, metal leaf, shellac, and many different resins for varnishes, which you will learn about in our book.

At a simpler level, there was and still is a vast amount of rustic furniture painting, which tends to use stylized motifs. The work often imitates the designs seen in grand houses, but uses simpler products and skills, such as those needed for stenciling, woodstaining, and liming. All of these authentic techniques can be replicated in your home.

The Artist's Techniques are in some ways the most difficult to categorize as the artist can be found working with the house painter, furniture painter, and restorer. In the past, the artists were primarily good draftsmen and colorists, who were employed to paint scenes on plaster, wall panels, and pieces of furniture. Some would have been full-time commercial painters, while others

Exciting effects can be achieved by combining a number of different materials on the same object. In decorating this obelisk (right), Kate Gwynn has used waxes, metal transfer leaf, and pigment.

would have used the work to supplement the income they gained from their private paintings. This section includes such classic finishes as fresco, glue painting, and patinating walls. Although these do require the skills of an artist if an intricate design is selected, they can also be practiced at a simpler level by almost anyone.

The Restorer's Techniques, which are aimed at simulating the character of antique furniture, is our final section. The restorer is concerned more with creating a traditional or aged look, than with actually using a classic technique. Particularly in recent years, there has been a general move away from making surfaces look new and fresh and toward giving them a distressed and timeworn character. Whereas cracked or peeled paint was previously seen as undesirable, it is now often thought of as a virtue. Techniques have been developed which can create these effects, such as antiquing and distressing, crackle varnish, and verdigris, giving surfaces a texture with a sense of applied history.

Kate Gwynn used the technique of oil-gilding to apply Dutch metal transfer leaf to the base of the obelisk (below). As a final touch she then added lines to the main body using a paint made with Venetian Red pigment (opposite).

The ease with which the materials featured in this book can be obtained depends greatly on what they are. The essential ingredient for all paintmaking is pigment, the coloring matter, and these are sold in some paint stores, or otherwise can be found at any good artist's supply store. Some paints can be made with materials found at home – simple milk paint and egg tempera for example. Other materials, such as whiting and lime putty, may be more difficult to find. Happily, an increasing number of small companies have been set up in response to the growing demand. As well as stocking the raw materials, they are now manufacturing their own specialty paints and other materials such as varnishes. There are now even reproduction historical paints, which, although using modern manufacturing techniques, use natural pigments and look and feel like the 18th- and 19th-century paints on which they are based.

The recent growth in the number of specialty manufacturers is a reflection of the paint revolution which has taken place over the past few years. We hope our book will go some way towards a greater understanding of the materials and techniques associated with this revolution. We hope, too, that the book will inspire and, above all, that you will enjoy trying out these techniques. As you become accustomed to using unfamiliar materials to create different effects and finishes, you will become aware of the exciting and endless possibilities for re-creating classical effects, or even using the materials and techniques to invent innovative, contemporary looks.

Annie Sloan
Kate Gwynn

The Paint and Equipment Directory

◆ *Mediums and Thinners* ◆
◆ *Oil-based Paints* ◆ *Water-based Paints* ◆
◆ *Artist's Paints* ◆ *Waxes and Woodstains* ◆
◆ *Varnishes, Gums, and Resins* ◆
◆ *Brushes* ◆ *Preparation* ◆ *Mixing Paint* ◆

PAINT'S MOST important purpose is to protect and preserve vulnerable surfaces, although this is often overlooked in favor of its secondary purpose of decoration. The quality of a paint is judged by the length of time the coating maintains its decorative and protective value. This varies according to the preparation and the condition of the original surface, how the paint is applied, and the suitability and quality of the paint itself. There are very many different types of paint – far more than most people realize – all with different applications and with many different textures. Apart from the generally available commercial paints, there are smaller manufacturers who make paint for a specialty market.

There are some basic rules for applying paint to ensure a good, long-lasting surface. Paints are either oil-based or water-based. Oil and water do not mix and nor do the paints based on them. It is possible to cover a water-based paint with an oil paint, but not vice versa. A latex/vinyl emulsion paint will not adhere to a gloss paint unless the gloss surface has first been sanded. Early painters prepared surfaces to turn out smooth, neat work using pumice, a volcanic rock still in use, dried shark skin, and horsetail (a plant) as abrasives. Absorbent surfaces should be primed with

Metals (right) have a particularly smooth surface and some, like iron, are prone to rust. For these reasons special paints have been produced which can adhere to and protect metal surfaces. Paints for metal should not be confused with metallic paints, which are paints made of metal suspended in a medium. Radiators used to be painted with metallic paints, which were thought to help conduct the heat, but nowadays they are simply painted with standard house paints.

either a recommended primer or a thinned down version of the subsequent coat.

In general, several thin coats of paint are better than one thick one, particularly with oil paints. Oily paints are referred to as "fat." In general, the first coat should be "thin," with subsequent layers of paint becoming "fatter." The exception is simple oil paint (*see pages 70–71*), which should be applied in alternate layers of "fat" and "thin" coats so that the "fat" coat feeds the "thin" coat.

A simple paint system is comprised of a priming coat, an undercoat, and a top or finishing coat. The priming coat ensures lasting adhesion to the surface, the undercoat provides a surface for subsequent coats to adhere to, and the topcoat gives color and the degree of finish. A current trend is to develop commercial paints which do not need primers or undercoats, thus making the job of painting both simpler and quicker for the home

In the nineteenth century, the training of house painters was taken very seriously. An apprenticeship could last seven years. Shown here (right) is a class of Dutch students in 1898. The feather and the two modern brushes, a chiqueter and a badger hair softener (above) are little changed from the equipment the students would have used.

In recent years there has been a renewed interest in classic products and particularly in those derived from plants. Here (left) a pine tree is being tapped for its oily resin. The resin, sometimes known as balsam, can then be distilled to produce turpentine and colophony/rosin, a product used in varnishes.

decorator. However, the ingredients of traditional undercoats and primers had specific uses. Gray undercoats contained graphite and white undercoats contained zinc oxide, both of which are waterproofing agents.

Modern oil paints are produced with three different finishes: gloss, semiflat/eggshell/mid-sheen, and flat/mat. Originally there was only one type of oil paint, which was made from a drying oil and pigment. It was used on paneling, doors, and other woodwork, just as oil paint is used today. Different oils were used in its manufacture, although the commonest paint was made from linseed.

Early water-based paints used to be called whitewash or calcimine/distemper; the term "paint" was reserved exclusively for oil paints. Water-based paints were made from powdered chalk, which acted as a base, water, and size, which bound the ingredients together. The finely ground chalk was often called Spanish White, and this term is frequently mentioned in the accounts books of grand houses. Today, the ground chalk is called whiting. Calcimine/distemper was a cheap paint which was easy to color simply by adding pigments.

Nowadays, water-based paints are sold as latex paints or vinyl emulsions, and are available in flat/mat and a variety of semiflat/mid-sheen finishes. A recent innovation is a water-based gloss finish. Modern paints may contain fillers, which increase the bulk of the paint and make it cheaper to produce. The filler in many commercial household paints is titanium dioxide, which has the additional advantage of increasing the brightness of the paint because it scatters light. Other additives are designed to prevent the paint from settling in the can, to stop the growth of bacteria, and to

control viscosity. Thickening agents are sometimes also used to produce "solid," thixotropic, nondrip latex/vinyl emulsion paints which are sold in trays.

Apart from cheap commercial paints, decorators also use paints which were primarily developed for the fine artist. In the past, the roles of the artist and decorator were not always clearly differentiated and the materials and equipment they used overlapped. These days, artist's paints and materials are generally used for high-quality, skilled work, as the paints are finer and purer (and more expensive) than decorating paints.

The rate of scientific discovery has accelerated since the 18th century and has had a growing impact on the development of paints. There have been spectacular changes in the paint industry during the last 100 years. To a large extent, modern paint manufacturers have responded to the demands of the home decorator, producing easy-to-use, plastic-based paints. Many of them, although different in name, look similar when used.

Since the removal of lead from domestic paints, commercial paints have become increasingly synthetic, like this gloss paint (top left). In the past, this gloss effect could only be achieved by varnishing lead-based oil paint. Plant-based paints, such as linseed oil-based paint (bottom left), have not disappeared completely. This one is known as two pot paint – one pot for the paint and one for the drier. The drier should only be added just before the paint is applied as otherwise it may become brittle and crack.

In the past, artists tended to specialize in one particular discipline, whether it was gilding, lacquering or varnishing, and they only used the tools and materials of their own particular trade. Today there is a far greater interchange of techniques and materials. Here (below) a large volume of paint was required by the fine artist and so a roller tray was used to mix the paint instead of the more conventional palette.

Mediums and Thinners

PAINT CONSISTS principally of a coloring agent, a medium, which binds the paint, and a thinner, which makes the paint more workable. Sometimes an additional medium is added to a paint to thicken it, extend it, or change the drying time. Unlike adding solvents or thinners, this has the advantage of changing the viscosity of paint without diluting it.

Paint may also contain thinners or solvents to make it less fat and improve its flow. They are also used to dilute paint and to clean brushes and other equipment. Just as paints, stains, and varnishes are water-, oil-, or spirit-based, so, correspondingly, are their solvents.

Beeswax
Wax (right) is used as a medium in a form of painting known as encaustic. The pigments are stirred into melted wax and the paint is then applied with a brush and with other tools.

Oil
Oil (below) is the most important medium in painting. Many types of oil have been used, but the commonest is linseed oil.

Egg yolk
Egg yolk (above) was used as a medium to make tempera by the Italian painters of the 14th and 15th centuries.

Hide/animal glue
Also known as size, animal glue (above) has been in use since ancient times and makes an excellent binding agent and sealer for paints.

Casein
Derived from nonfat milk solids, casein (right) is used with lime to make milk paint, or egg to make tempera.

Gum arabic
Gum arabic (above) is used as a binder for watercolor painting.

Lime
Lime (above) is an important medium in the history of paint. Lime (calcium oxide) results from heating limestone. It is also called quicklime, burnt lime, or caustic lime. Slaked lime is lime to which water has been added.

Polyvinyl acrylic/PVA
This product (above right) can be used as a glue, sealer, and binder with pigments to make paints.

Casein tempera binder
Casein is now also available ready-mixed (above).

Thinners and solvents
The usual thinner for oil paint is turpentine (far left). Water (center left) is the solvent for latex paints/vinyl emulsions, and acrylics. For spirit varnishes, such as shellac, use denatured alcohol/ methylated spirits (near left).

Turpentine

Water

Denatured alcohol/ methylated spirits

Linseed oil
Linseed oil (near and center right) is obtained from the seeds of the flax plant (far right). The cold pressing method produces an artist's quality oil. Boiled linseed oil and sun-bleached oil, which are quicker drying, are used for fine painting. Raw linseed oil, which is produced by steaming, is commonly used in exterior work.

Boiled linseed oil

Raw linseed oil

Flax

Driers
Driers, sometimes called siccatives, are metallic salts added to oil paints and varnishes to accelerate the drying rate. Light-drying oil (far left) and copal medium (center left) are used with artist's paints, and terebene driers (near left) with house paints.

Light-drying oil

Copal medium

Terebene drier

Dispersed glaze

Transparent oil glaze

Glazes
A glaze is a transparent medium into which pigment is mixed. It is then painted over a base. Dispersed glaze (above) is made by dispersing linseed oil in water. Acrylic scumble (near right) is made with acrylic resin. Oil glaze (far right) is made with linseed oil, driers, and resins.

Acrylic scumble glaze

Oil-based Paints

OIL-BASED paints are used mainly on woodwork, such as window frames and doors, and in areas which need frequent wiping, such as kitchens and bathrooms. The only oil-based paint used on walls is eggshell, which has a semigloss finish. Most oil-based paints are glossy to some degree, except for a flat/mat oil paint.

Oil-based paints have several advantages over water-based paints. In particular, they are stronger and more durable. The main disadvantages are that they take longer to dry between coats and brushes cannot be cleaned in water. All oil-based paints use either mineral spirits/white spirit or oil of turpentine as a solvent.

It is thought oil paints were developed to protect soft woods like pine which, unlike hard woods such as oak, are likely to be damaged without a protective coating.

The classic form of oil paint is a mixture of raw linseed oil, pigment, and driers. Other oils were also used, poppy and walnut oils, for example. Resin was added to the paint to make it glossier – presumably, more attractive and desirable.

Enamel paint
Based on varnish or varnish and oil mixtures, this paint (below) dries to an extremely hard, glossy surface. When it was developed in the 19th century, zinc oxide was used as a base. The use of machinery enabled the paint's components to be ground very finely to make it smooth.

Metal paint
This paint (left) is a tough, protective coating used for painting metal. It is made from resins, heat-hardened glass, and pigments. It has a fast-drying solvent and is touch dry in about 30 minutes. A special solvent is needed for cleaning brushes.

Floor paint
A very tough, hard-wearing paint (above), it often contains a high proportion of varnish. It is water-resistant and can withstand a lot of wear and tear.

Radiator/ heatproof paint
This paint (above) has been specially formulated to resist heat and changes in temperature. Enamel or floor paints are used for this purpose in the United States.

Japan paint
Japan is a loose term applied to a pigment suspended in an oil-free varnish or enamel. It (above) is a high-gloss paint, which can be used on metal. It originated from a 19th-century attempt to imitate oriental lacquer.

From antiquity until the early 20th century, white lead was the pigment that formed the principal basis of oil paints. Titanium dioxide, a dense, opaque white pigment, is in use today. Although highly toxic, lead makes a very strong paint, which, if properly applied, lasts for 20 years or more. Modern paints fail by cracking and flaking, but lead paints age beautifully. As the linseed oil dries out, the color changes, and the resulting effect is a patina – a slightly chalky appearance – quite unlike the look of modern paints. Early oil paints were uneven in both color and sheen and the pigments were often coarsely ground – not like the exacting uniformity of today's paints.

Exterior paints

Most exterior paints (right) are oil-based as these provide the best protection from the elements. Constant developments within the paint industry suggest that there will soon be equally durable water-based paints available.

Two pot paint

This (below right) is an old, natural paint based on linseed oil. It is available in two pots, one containing paint, the other containing a siccative, which is a terebene balsam drier of vegetable origin. The drier is added when the paint is used.

Eggshell

An oil paint (right) with a semigloss finish, it is used as a base for oil glazes.

Flat oil paint

An oil paint without any sheen (below), it was popular for interior work

Commercial gloss paint

This (right) is one of the commonest paints. A typical mix contains 60 per cent alkyd resin, 25 per cent titanium dioxide, and the rest mineral spirits/white spirit.

Natural gloss paint

This paint (right) uses linseed oil and natural resins to produce a high sheen. Many years ago there was no gloss paint, only lead-based oil paint. This had to be varnished if a gloss effect was wanted.

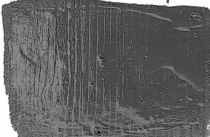

Lead paint

Today lead paint (above) is not available for residential use. In some countries, it can be used under special license to restore historic buildings and monuments.

Water-based Paints

WATER-BASED paints are quick drying, and the brushes used can be cleaned in water. However, they are not so strong as oil-based paints and, except for modern plastic paints, the painted surface cannot be washed.

These paints are commonly used as wall paints and have a long history. Most modern, commercial water-based paints are known as latex or vinyl emulsion paints. They consist of water and either polyvinyl acetate (hence vinyl) or acrylic polymers.

Today's mass-produced paints are based on polymers, which coat the surface with a film and eventually blister and flake.

Classic water-based coatings, such as limewash and calcimines/distempers, are absorbed into the surface and allow it to "breathe." The surfaces have a natural, chalky look and feel to them. "Reproduction" paints are now being manufactured to resemble classic paints in color and feel.

Until recently, there were no water-based gloss paints. There are now some commercially produced gloss paints, which are solvent-free and can be washed out of brushes with detergent and water.

Natural base plus color
This paint (right) is made with a concentrated, natural colorizer based on natural resins, vegetable and ethereal oils, and earth and mineral pigments. It can be added to any base.

Finnish cooked paint
This traditional Scandi-navian paint (right) is cheap and durable, last-ing from 30 to 50 years. It has been used in Sweden and Finland for centuries. It is made from rye and wheat flour boiled in water, iron sulfate, and earth pigments.

Limewash
This ancient coating (right) is made by slaking lime (see page 75). Its great advantage over modern paints is that it allows walls to "breathe," and water and salts from the wall to pass through. It does not peel and crack like plastic paints. When properly made, it will not powder when brushed against. It cannot be applied over an impervious surface.

Casein
Casein paint (left) is made from milk curds. Casein itself is often used in conjunction with other binders, such as lime or tempera, to strengthen it.

Soft calcimine/distemper
This (left) is a water-based paint using whiting, glue size as a binder, and pigments. When properly made, calcimine/distemper is not powdery.

Natural color stain and latex/vinyl emulsion
This (above left) has the same natural colorizer as the picture above, but in concentrated form and mixed with latex/vinyl emulsion.

Modern, water-based paints
Paints such as the one used on this wall (left) are commercially manufactured, modern water-based paints produced in large quantities. They are called latex in the United States and Europe, and vinyl emulsion paints in Britain. They are available in flat or semiflat finishes.

Oil-bound calcimine/distemper
This (below right) is calcimine/distemper to which oil has been added, yet it remains a water-based paint. (Similar liquids in which fat or oil is present are milk and mayonnaise.) When two immiscible liquids, such as oil and water, are mixed together, they form an emulsion.

Latex/vinyl emulsion
This is the name given to modern water-based paints (below right), particularly in the United States and Europe. Latex/vinyl emulsion is now also available as a thixotropic gel paint.

Mediterranean pigments
These nontoxic pigments are imported from Turkey and made into paint (left) by adding water.

Semigloss latex/vinyl silk
This (right) is a vinyl paint with a silk finish. These paints may be washed and scrubbed, and are very tough. There is a variety of finishes, such as flat/mat, semigloss and gloss.

Reproduction color
These (right) are modern paints which are made to look like old paints, such as buttermilk paints. They are based on historical colors.

Plaster plus pigment
This (above) is a plaster-like product with varying drying times. It can be painted on a wall and then sculpted with a trowel as it dries.

Artist's Paints

ARTISTS REQUIRE that paint remain permanent for hundreds of years, and for this reason artist's paints are purer and finer than decorator's paints. Artist's paints also differ from decorator's paints in that they are not standardized, so a Sienna, for example, will be brighter or duller depending upon the manufacturer. As some pigments are more liable to fade than others, most artist's paint companies produce a guide showing how permanent each pigment is.

In house decoration, artist's paints are used mainly for murals and painting furniture. There are two quality ranges of artist's colors, an artist's range and a cheaper, student's range. Although there is little perceptible difference between them, the artist's range does use finer, better quality pigments, and is more permanent.

Artist's paints can be oil paints, watercolors, or acrylic paints. Some people prefer oil paints because the different colors have more individual characteristics, such as their degree of transparency or opacity. Others prefer acrylics because the colors are more standardized and quick drying, making overpainting easier. Artist's paints may be bought ready made, but making your own teaches you about the inherent behavior of the pigments.

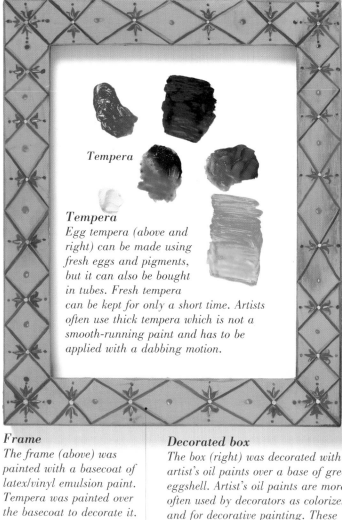

Tempera

Tempera
Egg tempera (above and right) can be made using fresh eggs and pigments, but it can also be bought in tubes. Fresh tempera can be kept for only a short time. Artists often use thick tempera which is not a smooth-running paint and has to be applied with a dabbing motion.

Oil paint
The most popular paint (right) since the 16th century, it is very versatile, and dries slowly with a slight sheen.

Oil paint

Oil paint mediums
There are numerous kinds of mediums for oil paints which change the paints' properties. They (right) can speed drying times, improve flow, add texture, gloss or mat finishes, and act as translucent extenders.

Oil paint medium

Frame
The frame (above) was painted with a basecoat of latex/vinyl emulsion paint. Tempera was painted over the basecoat to decorate it.

Decorated box
The box (right) was decorated with artist's oil paints over a base of green eggshell. Artist's oil paints are more often used by decorators as colorizers and for decorative painting. These paints are slow drying, which can be an advantage. Both turpentine and mineral spirits/white spirit can be used as a thinner.

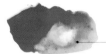

Watercolor

Watercolors

These (above) have a transparent quality and are rarely used on furniture or walls, as they must be waterproofed with varnish.

Gouache

Gouache (left) is a watercolor paint made with chalk to render it opaque. It is particularly useful for flat painting and must be oil-varnished for protection.

Gouache

Acrylic

Acrylic paints

Acrylics (above) are modern, water-based paints developed as an alternative to oils. They are very adaptable and can be applied in either thick or thin layers. Brushes should be washed in water immediately after use, as they cannot be cleaned once dry. These paints need not be varnished.

Gum arabic

Gum arabic (right) is used as a medium both to make watercolor and gouache paints, and to change their viscosity. It can be bought in liquid or in lump form. It was used on the drawing board (above right) to improve the viscosity of the paint so that it could be used with a dipping pen.

Gum arabic

Drawing board

This drawing board (above) was painted with two coats of latex/vinyl emulsion. It was decorated with inks, acrylic, watercolor, and gouache paints. The gouache and acrylic were mixed with gum arabic. The design was made using a dipping pen, not a brush, and was varnished with polyurethane.

Waxes and Woodstains

WAXES AND WOODSTAINS are decorative and protective finishes. Woodstains are transparent liquids applied to untreated wood which allow the natural grain of the wood to show through. There are three different types: oil stains, spirit stains, and water stains.

Waxes may be used on untreated wood or over surfaces that have already been painted or stained. Wax ages well and develops a patina as successive layers are built up. To make a solid, pure wax into a usable paste, melt the wax and mix it with turpentine to the proper consistency.

Carnauba
wax flakes

Carnauba
wax

Japan
wax

Maple wax

Liming wax

Liming
wax

Organic waxes
Japan wax (above) is extracted from the berries of the sumac tree. It is very fatty, feels oily, and is quite tough and flexible. It can be mixed with beeswax. Carnauba wax (above center and far right) comes from the leaf covering of a Brazilian palm. It is the hardest of all waxes, has the highest melting point, and will polish to a very high degree.

Maple
wax

Antique
pine wax

Colored waxes
These (above and right) include liming wax, a mix of whiting and beeswax, and maple and antique pine wax, which are colored with pigment to resemble wood tones.

Antique
pine wax

Nonorganic waxes
Waxes dug from the ground, known as earth waxes, include microcrystalline (near right) and paraffin (below). They are inexpensive.

Natural wax mix
This wax (center left) contains beeswax, carnauba wax, candelilla wax, citrus oil, and oil of turpentine, making it a soft, liquid wax.

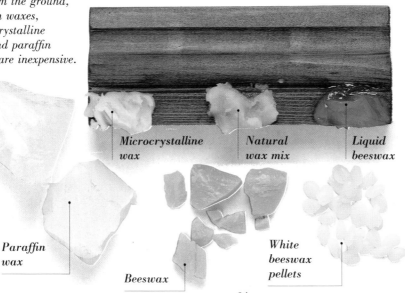

Microcrystalline
wax

Natural
wax mix

Liquid
beeswax

Beeswax
Made from the honeycombs of bees, beeswax is available in various forms (left), such as a liquid, a solid, and pellets. It is usually yellowish in color but transparent in use. Being very soft, it is often mixed with other waxes, such as carnauba, to make it stronger and less brittle.

Paraffin
wax

White
beeswax
pellets

Beeswax

Potassium
bichromate
crystals

Cloth
stained by
potassium
bichromate

Van Dyck
water-based
stain

Van Dyck
crystals

Potassium
bichromate

Blueberry
water-based
stain

Potassium bichromate
These crystals (top left) are mixed with warm water to make a stain. The crystals are toxic and must be handled with care.

Water-based stains
These water-based stains (above) are easy and practical to use; most people prefer them to those based on spirits or turpentine. Van Dyck crystals, made from walnut shells, give a light tan to deep brown color. Acrylic-based, water-based stains are available in a wide range of colors, including "Blueberry."

Oils
These oils (left) all enhance the natural grain of the wood. Teak oil both seals and feeds the wood. Traditional, natural furniture oil can be used on its own or as a base for wax polish, which will then give wood a natural shine. Tung oil is a natural nut oil, originally used for waterproofing Chinese junks and brought to the West in the late 19th century. It is useful in kitchens and bathrooms because it is waterproof.

Teak oil

Traditional,
natural
furniture oil

Dark oak
spirit-based
stain

Spirit-based stains
A variety of stains (above right and right) use denatured alcohol/methylated spirits or another alcohol as a solvent. They are volatile and dry quickly. The stain may be thinned by adding more spirits to make softer colors.

Tung oil

Mahogany
spirit-based
stain

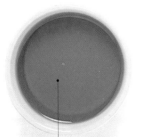

25

Varnishes, Gums, and Resins

NATURAL VARNISHES are made from the gums and resins collected from certain trees. Modern proprietary varnishes are based on synthetic resins. Resins are insoluble in water but dissolve in turpentine, oils, and spirits. Resins or gums used to be added to paint to make it spread better, dry quicker, and give a higher gloss. The blend of resin or gum with linseed oil became known as varnish. Varnishes are also called lacquers, but, strictly speaking, a lacquer is made from seedlac or lac, an animal resin. Most varnishes are soluble in turpentine. There were many different recipes for mixing gums to make specific varnishes, many of which are still in use today.

Some of the simplest varnishes, or rather lacquers, are those made from lac which has been dissolved in alcohol, such as denatured alcohol/methylated spirits. There are many different uses and grades of varnishes, each to be selected depending on its application.

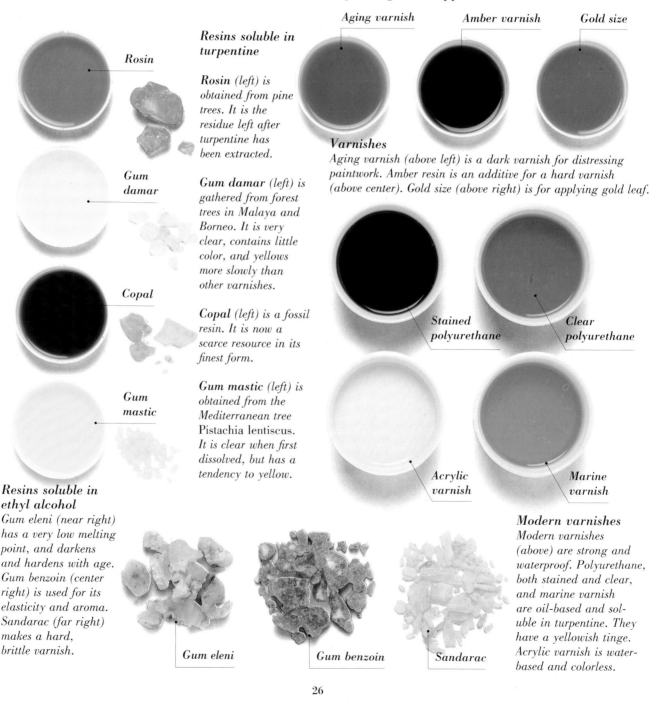

Resins soluble in turpentine

Rosin

Rosin (left) is obtained from pine trees. It is the residue left after turpentine has been extracted.

Gum damar

Gum damar (left) is gathered from forest trees in Malaya and Borneo. It is very clear, contains little color, and yellows more slowly than other varnishes.

Copal

Copal (left) is a fossil resin. It is now a scarce resource in its finest form.

Gum mastic

Gum mastic (left) is obtained from the Mediterranean tree Pistachia lentiscus. It is clear when first dissolved, but has a tendency to yellow.

Aging varnish   Amber varnish   Gold size

Varnishes
Aging varnish (above left) is a dark varnish for distressing paintwork. Amber resin is an additive for a hard varnish (above center). Gold size (above right) is for applying gold leaf.

Stained polyurethane   Clear polyurethane

Acrylic varnish   Marine varnish

Resins soluble in ethyl alcohol
Gum eleni (near right) has a very low melting point, and darkens and hardens with age. Gum benzoin (center right) is used for its elasticity and aroma. Sandarac (far right) makes a hard, brittle varnish.

Gum eleni   Gum benzoin   Sandarac

Modern varnishes
Modern varnishes (above) are strong and waterproof. Polyurethane, both stained and clear, and marine varnish are oil-based and soluble in turpentine. They have a yellowish tinge. Acrylic varnish is water-based and colorless.

**Denatured alcohol/
methylated spirits**

Seedlac

Shellac's basic ingredients
Shown here are denatured
alcohol/methylated spirits (top)
and seedlac (above). Seedlac is
the name given to sticklac (the
raw material), after it has
been cleaned, crushed, and
washed from much of the red
lac dye. These are the
two basic ingredients of
all shellacs.

Cembra lac

**Plant alcohol
thinner**

Cembra lac
This shellac (top) dries to a
silky finish and is used on furniture. Cembra oil is obtained
from the needles of the cembra
pine, which are steam-heated
so the oils evaporate. It is
shown here with a plant alcohol thinner that is distilled
from potatoes.

Blonde dewaxed shellac
This is used to make a
transparent finish (left),
known in Britain as
French polish.

Garnet shellac
First the seedlac is heated
and stretched into thin
strips. When cool, it is
broken into flakes (below).
A build-up of layers creates
a dark brown finish.

Button lac
This is the first stage of
making shellac. The lac is
heated, filtered through
muslin, and hardened
into small, button-shaped
discs (below). It makes
a golden brown finish.

Black polish
This is a very dark shellac
(left). It is derived from a
technique for making an
ebonizing stain, where
wood was colored with
Copperas, logwood chips,
or Verdigris, and then
coated with finely pow-
dered Indigo or Lamp-
black and shellac.

Brushes

OWADAYS WE TEND to use the same brush for several jobs, but in the past there was a different brush for every job, as brushes manipulate and disperse the paint in a variety of ways. In particular, water brushes have been distinguished from oil brushes.

A brush comprises the hair or bristles, the ferrule which binds them, and the handle. House painters' brushes tend to have a stock to which the brushes are attached by way of the ferrule. Handles may be separate or part of the stock. Many handles are round to facilitate intricate movement. The handles of both American and Continental-made brushes are not varnished; the handles of British brushes often are. Large wall brushes often have flat handles, usually pierced so that they may be hung up after use.

Soft hair for brushes comes from a variety of animals. The most popular are ox, squirrel, and sable, with badger for more specialist work. The finest brushes are made from sable; the coarsest are probably floggers made with bristle. An alternative type of sable brush is made of squirrel hair, sometimes called camel hair, which is rather confusing! Bristle is a tougher material used for oil work and emulsion. Hog bristle and horsehair are used. The finest hog bristle is bleached and known as white or lily bristle.

Block brush
This brush (below) is used for walls. Its rectangular shape will hold a lot of paint.

Latex/vinyl emulsion brush
This (left) has a copper ferrule to avoid rust. Nowadays a mixture of synthetic filaments and bristle, originally it was a mixture of natural fiber and bristle.

Calcimine/ distemper and limewash brush
Made of plant fiber, the brush (right) is soaked in water before use to make it soft. It is good for large, uneven walls, especially exterior surfaces.

Paint roller
This example (right) has a mohair sleeve. Rollers are very popular because they can cover a large surface area quickly.

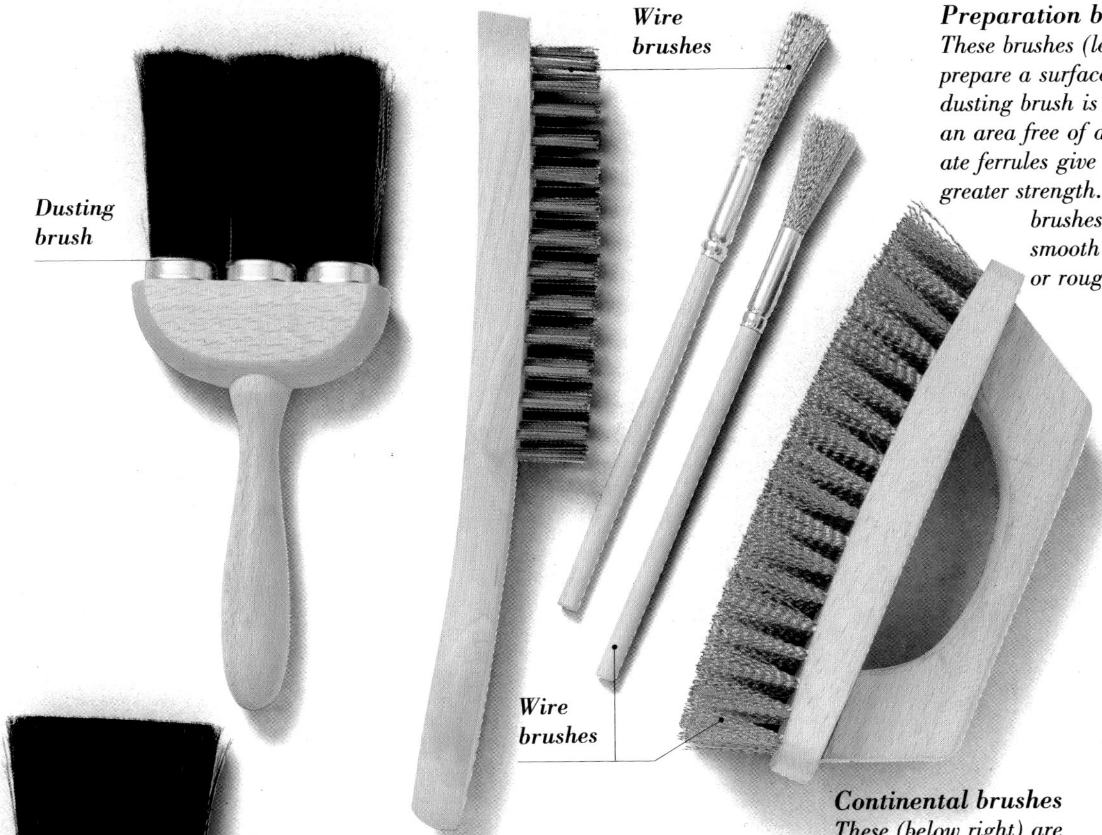

Dusting brush

Wire brushes

Preparation brushes
These brushes (left) are used to prepare a surface for paint. The dusting brush is used to sweep an area free of dust. The separate ferrules give the hairs greater strength. The four wire brushes are used to smooth out an uneven or rough surface.

Wire brushes

Continental brushes
These (below right) are used for oil painting. They come in various shapes, domed, pointed and round, but are all characteristically round-ferruled. The yellow string bridle can be moved down as the brush wears down. This shape is seen only in glue brushes in the United States and Britain.

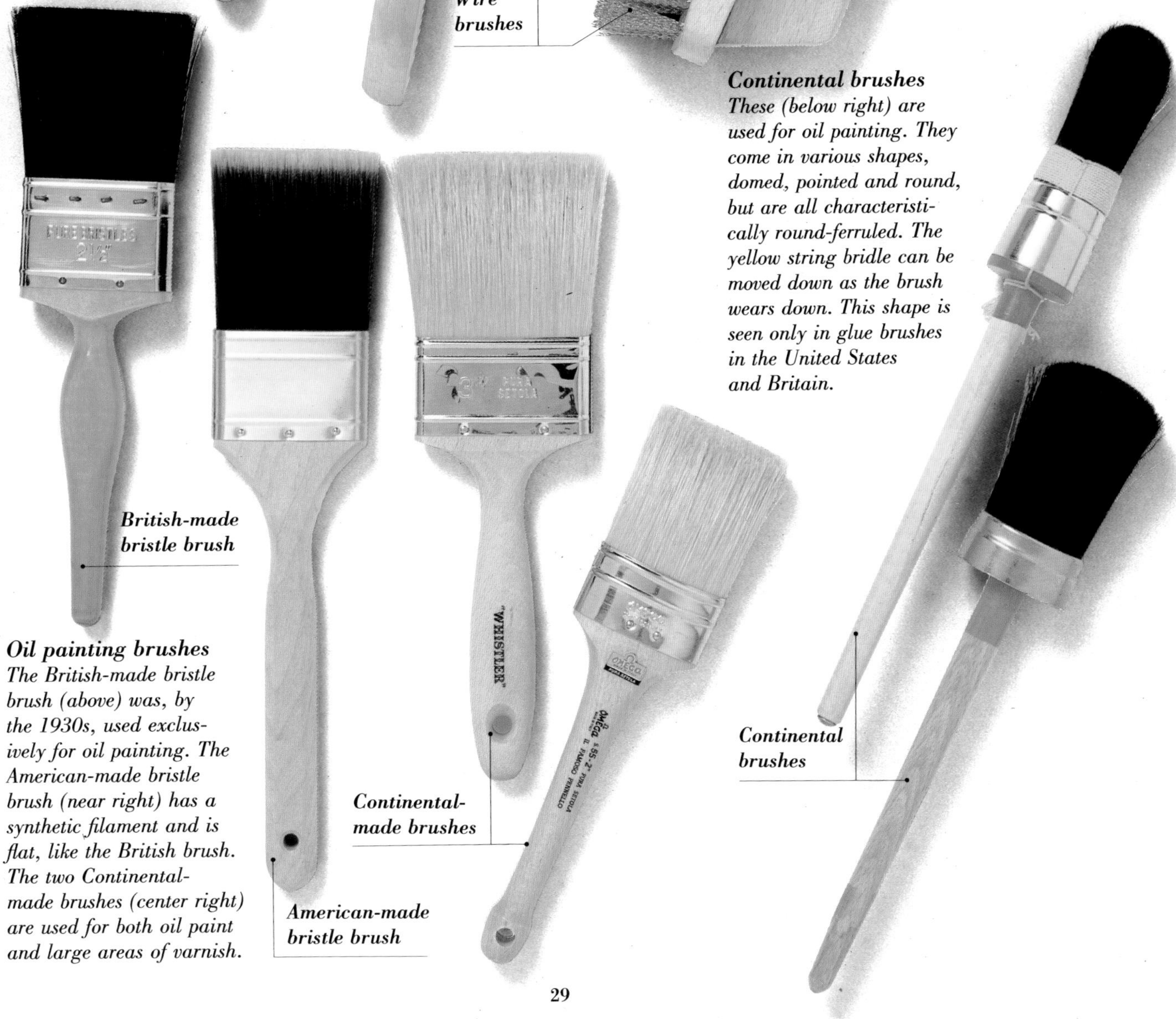

British-made bristle brush

Continental-made brushes

Continental brushes

Oil painting brushes
The British-made bristle brush (above) was, by the 1930s, used exclusively for oil painting. The American-made bristle brush (near right) has a synthetic filament and is flat, like the British brush. The two Continental-made brushes (center right) are used for both oil paint and large areas of varnish.

American-made bristle brush

Copper-ferruled sash tool

Artist's brushes

Stencil brushes

Bristle pencil overgrainer

Bristle strié brush/dragger

Bristle mottler

Hog bristle brushes

A copper-ferruled sash tool (top) is a Continental house painter's brush now also used by artists all over the world. The three artist's brushes (above), called fitches, are for oil or acrylic. They may be flat, round, or filbert point (not shown), and vary in size and length of bristle.

Stencil brushes

There are several types of stencil brush (above), but they all have short bristles cut to give a flat edge. The brush (above right) is intended for water work and so has no ferrule to rust.

Woodgraining tools

This (left) is a selection of the many tools available. A bristle pencil overgrainer for oil work is used to highlight the figuring at the second stage of wood-graining. A bristle mottler has the same use. The bris-tle strié brush/dragger's use is as its name suggests.

Decorative brushes

The wide brush (below) is a bristle strié brush/dragger with the hair cut out at intervals to give stripes in graining. The other is for strié/dragging and flogging.

Squirrel hair mop

Synthetic hair brush

Mongoose hair brush

Sable brush

Ox hair brush

Chiqueter

Bristle strié brush/dragger

Badger hair softener

Goose feather

Hog's hair softener

Brush for strié/dragging and flogging

Other artist's brushes

Shown here (above) are a cheap squirrel hair mop for washes and shellacs; a top-range, all-purpose, synthetic hair brush; a mongoose hair brush, mainly for water work; a sable brush, also used for water work; and an artist's ox hair brush.

Marbling tools

This (above left) is a selection of the many tools available: a hog's hair softener for blending oil work; chiqueter, a squirrel hair brush arranged in three clumps which form points when wet; a badger hair softener for blending oil and water work. Goose feathers, taken from left and right wings, give different veining effects.

Squirrel hair swordliner

Long-haired lining brush

Angular lining fitch

Badger hair fan

Lining brushes
Lining brushes (right) are used to make lines on walls and furniture. Although the four quill writers were originally called after the actual bird's feather used, their names — from left to right, lark, crow, duck, and goose — now refer to the size of the brush/ferrule. The long-haired lining brush is made of oxette (cattle ear) and the angular lining fitch is a bristle brush for robust work in oil.

Quill writers

Fresco brushes
The badger hair fan and squirrel fan (right) are both for water work to make a wide sweep with a wash in fresco and tempera. The bristle fan (right) is for oil work and the two brushes used for fresco and gesso work (below right) have their string removed before use.

Bristle fan

Squirrel fan

Brushes for fresco and gesso work

Wax brushes
Here are a small round brush for applying wax to an intricate carving (below left); a polishing brush for attaching to power tools (below right); and a very soft brush for polishing delicate work (bottom).

Glue brush
The wire on this brush (left) helps to keep the hairs firm when applying thick and viscose glue.

Bristle brush

Squirrel hair brushes

Wax brush for intricate work

Polishing brush for power tools

Stippling brush
Made of bristle, these (below) come in many sizes and are used for decorative glaze work.

Varnish brushes
The brush (above left) is a bristle brush for varnish. The other brushes (above center and above right) are very soft, squirrel hair brushes for delicate lacquer and varnish work.

Polishing brush for delicate work

Preparation

REPARATION IS often the most time-consuming aspect of decoration, but to achieve a good finish it is important to prepare the paint surface properly. Take care not to inhale dust when rubbing down old paintwork, as the old paint may be lead-based which is toxic. Old wax can be removed by scrubbing with spirits and steelwool, or, alternatively, a commercially available wax remover could be used.

Cracked plaster should be filled with a prepared filler or homemade putty. One recipe, sometimes called Swedish putty, uses gloss or lead paint, whiting, and glue size.

Abrasives
There are many different types of abrasive (right). Sandpaper comes in various forms and grades. It can be used dry for rubbing down wood and some other surfaces or "wet and dry" for rubbing down paint. The water prevents the paper from being clogged up with fine particles. Steelwool, available in a range of grades, can be used to rub in wax or to rub down paintwork or other surfaces to an ultra-smooth surface. Finer abrasives are rottenstone, which is used with oil to polish surfaces, and pumice, used with soap, water, and a cloth on shellac to give a very smooth surface.

Cloths and tack cloths
A tack cloth (below right) removes dust and grease from a surface and is used to prepare surfaces in gilding. Cotton cloths (below) are used for wiping down and cleaning. Only cotton cloths should be used, as they are absorbent.

Rottenstone

Sandpapers

Pumice

Steelwool

Sandpaper pad

Tack cloth

Sugar soap

Cotton cloth

Fuller's earth

Wood bleach
This product (above) is used for bleaching wood after existing stains and dyes have been removed.

Cleaning agents
Sugar soap (above left) and fuller's earth (left) are degreasing agents used to wash down and prepare painted surfaces. Fuller's earth is also an abrasive.

Tools
Many different tools and materials are used in preparation (below). Masking tape is useful for protecting existing surfaces and carpets. Spatulas are used for filling chips, cracks, and nail holes. A chalk line is used for marking long, straight lines.

Spatula

Masking tape

Chalk line

Wood sealer/knotting
Wood sealer/knotting (right) is used to seal resinous new wood, so that resin does not seep out and lift the paint surface.

Fillers/putties
Fillers/putties are available ready-mixed (below right) or in powder form (below). They are used to fill holes and cracks in plaster walls and woodwork.

Wood sealer/ knotting

Ready-mixed filler/putty

Powdered filler/putty

Palette knife

Natural primer

Primers and undercoat paints
Primers (right) are used to ensure lasting adhesion to the surface and as sealers. Metal primers are based on Red Oxide. The commonest color in America in the 17th and early 18th centuries was a dark red called Spanish Brown. It was nearly always used for exterior painting and was often the only paint applied. Old primers were based on either white or red lead. Here a natural primer (top), a reproduction primer (center), and an aluminum primer (bottom) for use on wood and metal are shown. The natural primer contains linseed oil and cobalt zirconium. The reproduction primer is lead free, but looks and behaves very much like old-fashioned primer. Undercoat paints are applied over the primer to provide a "bed" for the topcoat.

Natural primer

Reproduction primer

Undercoat paints

Aluminum primer

Mixing Paint

MANY PEOPLE buy their paints ready-mixed in cans according to the manufacturer's color charts. But even with the vast range offered in shops where paint is mixed up for you, it is still not always possible to buy the exact color you are looking for. Besides, it is satisfying to mix your own colors and, once the basic rules are understood, not difficult.

Paint basically consists of a binding agent, such as linseed oil (or in the case of modern latex/vinyl emulsion a polymer), a solvent, such as turpentine or water, and a coloring agent, the pigment.

Paint can be made from its basic ingredients by mixing the binder and color together. There are many different binders – milk, chalk, egg, vegetable oils, wax – in fact, anything that sticks the pigment particles together and adheres to the surface to which it is applied. The binder's suitability depends on the amount of paint needed and the surface to be coated. Whether it produces a good paint depends on how long it lasts. Instructions for making paint can be found throughout the book.

For making large quantities it may be more convenient to use a ready-made base, like a white latex/vinyl emulsion or a white oil paint, and add your own color. Polyvinyl acrylic/PVA may also be used as a base, but it will dry to a transparent glaze. Adding whiting to the mixture will make it opaque. It is easier to add color to white, but coloring agents may also be added to colored bases.

There are a variety of coloring agents. Any artist's paint may be used to add color as long as it is compatible with the base. Artist's oil paint should be added only to oil-based paint, and acrylic should be added to a water-based paint. Coloring agents, such as universal stainers, which

Materials and equipment
A pestle and mortar are needed only for very fine work. Pigments differ in how much oil they absorb and whether they cover the surface well. The amount of pigment needed naturally depends also on the strength of color required.

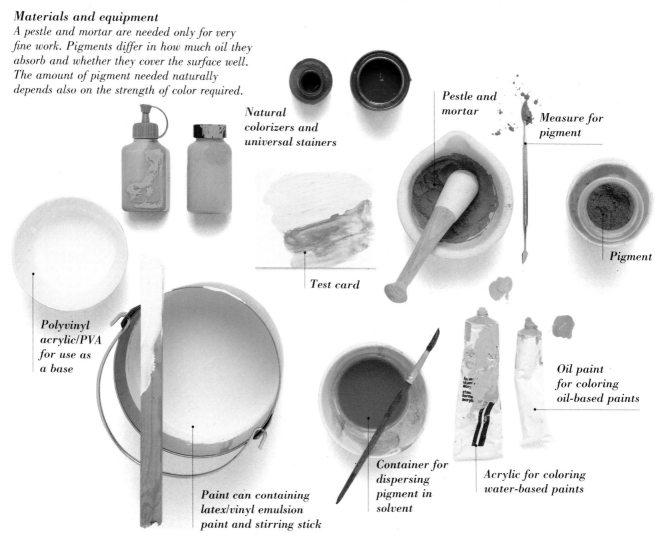

Natural colorizers and universal stainers

Pestle and mortar

Measure for pigment

Pigment

Test card

Polyvinyl acrylic/PVA for use as a base

Oil paint for coloring oil-based paints

Paint can containing latex/vinyl emulsion paint and stirring stick

Container for dispersing pigment in solvent

Acrylic for coloring water-based paints

are dyes, and dry powder pigments, may be added to both water-based and oil-based paints.

The advantages of using pigments, as opposed to commercial, ready-mixed paints, are that the color is often more intense and they can be added to any type of paint. They give the craftsman a feeling of being closer to the true nature of the pigment. They are the purest form of color, with no added fillers, so results are almost guaranteed. They are also intense, so a little pigment goes a long way.

We have come to expect uniformity from commercially produced paints. Every can contains the same color and it spreads in an even color under the brush. Paints were originally very uneven since the pigments were ground by hand.

There are two ways of adding color to paint. The simplest is to stir a powder into the paint. However, even when all the pigment appears to be dispersed evenly into the paint, small amounts will stick together; these become apparent only under the brush. This makes a slightly uneven coat which is much closer to the way paint used to look.

If a more even paint is required, the pigment should be added to just enough thinner to disperse it, and shaken in a glass jar. This disperses it evenly, and it can then be stirred into the base.

As the properties of different pigments vary, it is impossible to give general measures for the amount of pigment required. This can really be learned only through practical experience.

MIXING PIGMENT AND PAINT

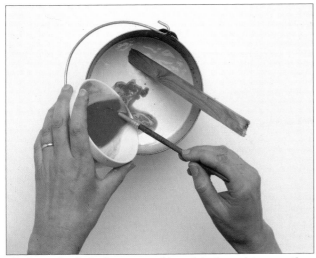

1 Measure out some pigment, in this case Raw Sienna. If necessary, a pestle and mortar can be used to grind it for fine work.

2 Add the pigment to water. Oil paint, acrylics, or universal stainers could also be used and should be diluted with the appropriate thinner.

3 Pour the desired amount of latex/vinyl emulsion or oil paint into a paint can and add some of the color.

4 Stir thoroughly until the color is dispersed throughout. Add more color and repeat the process until the desired shade is reached. Use a test card to check.

The Color Directory

♦ *Earth Pigments* ♦

♦ *Mineral Pigments* ♦ *Plant Pigments* ♦

♦ *International Palettes* ♦

♦ *Color Mixing* ♦

ART OF THE experience of visiting other countries is in viewing the colors of the buildings that we see there, which give a distinctive flavor to our memories. These colors define a nation, and can differentiate north from south as in France and the United States.

When visiting New England, no one can fail to be charmed by the array of brown-red barns and pale blue, gray, and ocher-painted houses. In Mexico, the colors are lively and extrovert combinations of vivid earth reds and yellows juxtaposed with brilliant greens and vibrant blues.

The variety in Europe is endless. From Belgium and Holland through Germany to Scandinavia, a specific very dark green is used on front doors, shutters, and window frames, set against red brickwork, warm earth colors, or white limewash. Scandinavia is also characterized by serene gray-blues; in recent years, these shades have influenced craftsmen in other countries, particularly when painting furniture. The stunning dusky, earthy pinks of Italy have long been an inspiration to many, while in Greece, Spain, and Portugal there are dazzling buildings painted with limewash white, often with a touch of clear blue.

All countries use earth colors, especially Oxide Reds and Yellow Ochers, which have always been cheap and plentiful. These color tones differ slightly from one country to the next – sometimes being warmer or deeper.

Color was used as a visible demonstration of increased social status, as pigments were priced differently. Thus, the house painter would charge according to the desired color. This price distinction remains today in the case of pure pigments or artist's color. Ordinary house paints now all cost the same, no matter what color, as they are made from synthetic dyes instead of pigments.

A price list from the 18th century, when only pigments were available, offered a ''fine deep green'' at eight times the cost of such colors as cream lead, pearl, and stone. Blue, certain oranges, lemon, and olive were also expensive colors that would give distinction to your house if chosen as wall colors. In Holland, at about the same time, black pitch was used on exterior wood-work, but as the owners grew wealthier, they would have this painted deep green – the more

These jars of pigment (left) are arranged on shelves in a store in Morocco. Dry pigment can still be bought in hardware stores in some countries, and from specialty artist's supply stores in others. In different regions of the world, pigments are mixed in different quantities to provide variations in their basic hue (below).

expensive option. Even early in this century, before commercial, mass-produced paints became accepted, house painters charged according to the color chosen, although, by then, there were many more cheap synthetic alternatives.

The choice of colors today is enormous, but perhaps a little bewildering to many. The same color chart may present bright primaries next to the palest pastels or deep shades. Some of the large companies offer a choice of thousands of shades, all different by a minute percentage of color. These paints are sometimes useful in obtaining a very precise color, but they do have a certain uniformity and standardization. For this reason, there has been a move in recent years toward small companies producing specialized colors with a particular characteristic, whether historic or geographic,

The huge choice of colors seen in commercial manufacturers' color charts (left) can sometimes be daunting and confusing. It is difficult to imagine the effect of a color in a room after seeing only a small swatch. When choosing a color, find a sample several tones darker to get an idea of the final shade.

such as a New England range of colors or a Mediterranean palette of colors.

In our everyday lives, brilliant colors are available at every turn, all competing for our attention. Bright color is in the street on cars, clothes, and billboards, and at home on packages, magazines, and plastic goods. We are drenched in bright color and long for a break from this constant bombardment and so seek the less demanding, more soothing, and subtler colors of the past. This is in direct contrast to the medieval world, when people's lives were surrounded by faded and muddied shades and they longed for colors that would bring clarity and brightness. They held the bright, clear red of Vermilion in high esteem, although its cost meant that even those who could afford it only used it in small quantities. The painters of illuminated manuscripts would search for these brilliant colors and even now, there is a jewel-like quality to these colors.

Today, enthusiasts for historic color search for clues about authentic color, and ideas are changing

In the past, "blue bags," which contained a very strong blue pigment, used to be added to the last rinse of white laundry to make the fabrics whiter. Here (above), the same pigment has been added to a small amount of white latex/vinyl emulsion paint and painted on a cardboard box. This makes an intense blue paint very cheaply. The wooden walls of early American houses were sometimes decorated in this way.

Houses in the United States are sometimes painted in a whole variety of different colors (above). These have been given the charming sobriquet of "painted ladies."

all the time. Information is obtained from painters' books, a few of which date from the 17th and 18th centuries and more from the 19th century. Also, scrapings are taken from old buildings to see the types of colors used under layers of paint. This technique can give rise to misconceptions. Undercoats are revealed and these may be misconstrued as the finished layer, or a color may have darkened or faded over the years. This seems to have happened particularly with certain greens, called Blue and Green Verdite, sometimes known as Bremen Blue or Green, made from copper. Where the scrapings revealed this pigment, the color was seen as a faded or dirtied green. In fact, when the color was first used it would have been quite a bright, clear, possibly even peppermint green color. Despite this, many people prefer to see old houses decorated in faded or muted colors as they associate these with an authentic look.

The history of color in houses and decorative work was not well documented, as it was in the hands of busy craftsmen rather than men of letters. Nowadays, the interest in color has been revived with the help of historians, conservationists, and artists who realize the need to understand and use authentic colors – the colors of the past.

Earth Pigments

THESE ARE very simple pigments found in the earth. In general, they are cheap and plentiful, but some deposits, such as those of Sienna in Tuscany, are scarce or even exhausted. The origin and use of these pigments can be traced across the world from the caves of Lascaux in the Dordogne, France, to South African rock paintings, and aboriginal paintings in Australia.

Traditional house decoration was often based on chalk or lime into which local pigments had been mixed, and today earth pigments continue to be of great importance in both the artist's and the decorator's palettes. Colors may vary slightly, according to the geographical areas in which the pigments are found, but their basic characteristics and properties remain the same.

Green clay

Yellow Ocher
This natural earth (below right) is a clay colored by iron, and occurs in a variety of earthy yellow shades. It is a warm, universal color.

Green Earth
This natural green clay color (above), containing small amounts of iron and manganese, varies from gray-green to olive green, depending on where it is found. It occurs in various locations in Europe and is a popular color in Italian fresco painting.

Chalk White
Calcium carbonate (above), also known as whiting, is an early, easily obtainable pigment made from chalk (below). As it does not retain its color when mixed with oil, it has been superseded mainly by titanium.

Black
There are different types of black pigment (above). Early, basic ones were obtained from carbon.

Chalk

Sandstone
This stone (above) contains deposits of yellow earth which can differ in color.

A red to purplish colored clay

Raw Umber
A natural earth pigment (above) made from manganese, it is a dark, cold color. When mixed with a white, it becomes a greenish gray.

Burnt Umber
This warm, red-brown (above) is made from roasting Raw Umber in furnaces. The best quality pigment originated from Umbria, Italy, but it now comes from Cyprus or Turkey.

A greenish cold colored clay

Indian Red
This Red Oxide (right) was formerly from India, but the term was also used by early American painters to describe an earth color used by Native Americans. Sometimes called Caput Mortuum, it is a purplish, cold red.

Burnt Sienna
A warm, red-brown color, it (below) is made by calcining or burning Raw Sienna.

Venetian Red
Originally one of the brightest red earths, containing 15 to 40 per cent iron oxide, it (above) is now produced artificially.

Terracotta tile
Clay containing iron oxide is baked to make tiles which vary in color from light orange (below) to rich brown-reds.

Raw Sienna
A pigment (left) made from a natural clay, it contains iron oxide and manganese. It absorbs a large amount of oil and is found worldwide.

Light brown clay

41

Mineral Pigments

MINERALS HAVE BEEN a source of coloring matter since ancient times. There were five main minerals used, in their cleaned and powdered form. These are no longer used because they are either prohibitively expensive, such as lapis lazuli, or they have been superseded. They are azurite and malachite, both copper minerals of blue and green, orpiment, a brilliant yellow, cinnabar, a bright red, and lapis lazuli, a clear blue.

Other colors could be made by using simple chemistry. Alchemists in the Middle East experimented with many materials in their search for precious metals. By mixing mercury and sulfur, they produced Vermilion, a bright red that replaced Cinnabar.

Copper was the most important metallic element, giving colors that the earth could not – Verdigris and various Lime Blues, sometimes called Verdite or Bremen Blue or Green. They were made using mixtures of copper sulfate and ammonia, and sometimes lime and Verdigris, to make various colors from blue through to green. There was also the poisonous copper arsenite, Emerald Green, which might be responsible for giving green its reputation as an unlucky color.

From the 18th century onward, a large number of cheaper and more reliable colors were discovered by chemists. These included Prussian Blue, Cobalts, Ultramarine, Cadmiums, Chromes, Alizarins and Manganese.

Copper
Verdigris (below right), an early artificial pigment, was unreliable but more easily available than malachite. It was a basic copper pigment produced by sandwiching copper sheets between grapeskin crushings, apple cider, or acetic acid. Phthalocyanine Blue and Green are relatively recent discoveries; they were first introduced in the 1930s and have superseded copper blues and greens.

Azurite

Verdigris

Phthalocyanine

Malachite

Viridian

Copper

Prussian Blue

Viridian
Viridian (above), a very bright, transparent emerald shade, was synthesized from chromium hydroxide, a synthetic, inorganic pigment made of potassium bichromate and boric acid.

Prussian Blue
A deep greenish blue, this pigment (above) was discovered in 1704 by a chemist attempting to make artificial crimson from iron salt, potash, and blood.

Chrome
A number of artificial pigments (right), ranging from pale yellow to deep orange-scarlet, are obtained from lead chromates. Chrome Yellow was discovered by Vauquelin in Paris in 1797, and has been commercially manufactured since 1818. Since its discovery, a number of other chrome pigments have been developed. Chrome Green, for example – also known as Brunswick Green, Prussian Green, and Cinnabar Green – was made from Chrome Yellow and Prussian Blue. All chrome pigments are slightly toxic.

Chrome Yellow

Chrome Orange

Chrome Green

Manganese Violet

Manganese Black

Manganese Blue

Manganese
Manganese dioxide is the base for these pigments (left and above). Manganese Blue was invented at the beginning of the 20th century. Manganese Black and Manganese Violet are less common.

Cadmium

Cadmium was not discovered until 1817. It is a slightly toxic, silvery metal which was first found in zinc mines. It offers a wide range of pigments (right and below) within the red-yellow band of the color spectrum.

Cadmium Red-Purple

Cadmium Yellow-Lemon

Cadmium Yellow-Orange

Cadmium Red

Cadmium Yellow Deep

Flake White

Lead

Red Lead

Lead

Flake White (above), also called Lead White or Kremnitz White, was made by the stack method. Clay pots containing vinegar were stacked with horse manure, tanner's bark, or grapeskins to provide carbon dioxide and warmth. This corroded the lead to form lead carbonate, which was then washed, dried, and ground. White Lead dust is poisonous. Red Lead (above right), sometimes called Minium, is one of the oldest synthetic pigments.

Alizarin

This is a synthetic, organic color derived from coal tar, and comes in shades from scarlet to maroon (below and below left).

Alizarin Crimson

Alizarin Madder Light

Ultraviolet

Ultramarine

Lapis lazuli

Ultramarine

True Ultramarine was originally finely ground lapis lazuli (above far right). The French government offered a prize for a cheap replacement and it was won by Guimet in 1828 with French Ultramarine (above right).

Cerulean Blue

Cerulean Blue (below right) is a slightly cooler blue than Cobalt Blue and has a greenish tinge. It is an artificial mineral pigment made from heating cobalt sulfate with tin salts and silica.

Cerulean Blue

Asphaltum

Asphaltum

Asphaltum (left) is made from asphalt and is used to simulate age.

Zinc White

Zinc White (below) is an artificial pigment made by burning metallic zinc vapor. It is a nontoxic, semiopaque, cold white.

Zinc White

Zinc

Cobalt Violet

Cobalt Blue

Cobalt

Cobalt Blue (left) is a metallic element discovered in the latter part of the 18th century. The word cobalt comes from kobold meaning "goblin of the mines." Cobalt is used in the manufacture of blue glass and ceramic pigments. Cobalt Violet (far left) is made either from cobalt and arsenic (highly toxic) or from cobalt phosphate (nontoxic).

43

Plant Pigments

COLORS DERIVED from plants are not strictly pigments; they are dyes, which are manufactured from parts of the plant or from resins exuded by them. The difference is that the coloring substance of a dye is completely dissolved in the binder, while pigments are finely ground solids suspended in the binder. The Egyptians found a method of dissolving vegetable dyes in water and fixing the color to make a "lake." Paints made from plants usually have the word "lake" in their names, such as Scarlet Lake and Crimson Lake.

Plant dyes or lakes are not as permanent as some pigments. They are used mainly to produce color for fabric and wool dyes and for decorative

purposes in dyeing wood and coloring limewash. In general, they are too unstable for artists' use, but have been used widely for decorative purposes. Gamboge and dragon's blood are resins derived from natural sources such as trees, fruit, and roots, and were used to color clear varnishes.

As with pigments, many plant colors came from local sources. Many old recipes involve boiling bark, nuts, and roots to extract the color, while some combine ingredients to make other colors.

Dragon's blood
This (left), sometimes called Cinnabar, is a powdered form of a ruby red resin. It is often used to color varnishes.

Sanderswood chips
Derived from a large Indian tree of the sandalwood family, these (below right) produce yellow-red to deep crimson colored dyes. The color depends on the acidity of the mordant.

Gamboge
A yellow resin from Thailand, gamboge (left) has a transparent color which fades in bright light. Nevertheless, it has been in use from medieval times to the 19th century. It has now been largely replaced by Cobalt Yellow.

Fustic chips
These (right) come from a small tropical American tree, and make a yellow dye. In spite of its color, it was confusingly called Dutch Pink, Brown Pink, English Pink, and Stile Grain.

Charcoal
Charcoal is made from charred willow and beech tree twigs (left).

Barberry bark
Boiled in water, barberry bark (above) gives one of the few good yellow stains, in that it is strong and fairly permanent.

Logwood chips
Logwood chips (above) come from the inner core of a tree native to South and Central America. They were used unsuccessfully as a dye for cloth in 16th-century England, and are now used to make a red stain for wood.

Catechu powder
This (left) is made from boiling the heartwood of the acacia catechu tree in water. The water is strained, left to evaporate, and dried in molds.

Indigo

Indigo was first obtained from the tinctoria plant (below) grown in India, China, and Europe. It produces a transparent, deep violet-blue dye, mainly used on fabric. To make the powder the leaves are soaked in water until they ferment. On drying, the extract turns indigo. It is then washed, boiled, and dried.

Dried tinctoria plant

Turmeric

Extracted from the root of a spice plant, turmeric (above) is used to color varnishes, oils, and wax, and as a dye. It makes a fairly permanent, strong bright yellow color.

Indian Yellow

True Indian Yellow is an obsolete color, but a synthetic (above) is now manufactured, and Hansa Yellow and Cobalt Yellow are used as alternatives. Originally, it was made in India from the urine of cows fed on mango leaves.

Indigo

Madder

Madder (below) is available in root or powder form and makes a cool bluish red. It produces one of the best red plant dyes and has had a far-reaching influence as a color in both fabrics and paint. Madder Red, a warm crimson, and Rose Madder, a delicate but intense pink, are made from the plant but are not very permanent. Madder was used as a paint until the end of the 19th century.

Alkanet

Oil stained by alkanet

Alkanet

Alkanet (above) is a European plant giving a fine crimson color. For a good red oil for rubbing discolored mahogany or rosewood, tie some alkanet root in a muslin bag and let it soak overnight in the oil. Squeeze the bag to release the stain into the oil, which can then be rubbed on the wood.

Rose Madder

Madder twigs

Madder roots

Madder Red

International Palettes

APART FROM colors derived directly from pigments, many of today's paint colors take their inspiration from sources such as wallpapers, fabrics, and china. From the Orient, such products as blue china, gray-green Celadon porcelain and jade, indigo-blue chintz, orange-pink *Famille Rose* china, and clear yellow Chinese wallpaper have provided the West with a wealth of colors. Grand Tour visits to Greece and Rome introduced the purples and lilacs used in Aubusson and Gobelin tapestries and *toile de Jouy* fabrics. The great porcelain factories developed ceramic glazes giving now-famous colors, such as the Sèvres blue and Wedgwood's gray-blue.

Influences on paint color
This is a collection of color charts, fabrics, and ceramics which helps to demonstrate the influence that related decorative arts and artefacts have had on paint palettes and color schemes.

HC87

HC67

HC41

HC47

HC109

HC111

HC113

IF YOU LOOK at the use of color on vernacular buildings all over the world, it seems, at first, to show wide variations in the use of pigments. Closer inspection will reveal that the same basic pigments are used again and again, but in different guises. Only the choice of paint, the particular combination of colors, and variations in the exact pigments differ.

Apart from white, which appears on both walls and woodwork throughout the world, the main colors used are the warm earth reds and yellows. The earth pigments would, at one time, have been found locally and were cheap and plentiful. When you are traveling through some country regions, you might notice that the soil is a rich red or that the stone is yellow; it is likely that deposits of red oxide or ocher will be found. These are the sources of native pigments.

Sometimes colors would be imported by pigment suppliers and they were often known by their countries of origin – English Red, Spanish Red, Indian Red, French Ocher, and Sienna are all slight variations in the essential red oxide or ocher pigment. English Red, for instance, was imported into Continental Europe because it was a particularly clear and clean red with only a little trace of the earthy brown or manganese purple color found in some red oxides. The pigment was also used to color white limewash, resulting in beautiful mellow pink English farmhouses. Indian Red, sometimes

South Portugal

A clear blue, possibly a Lime Blue, outlining the window and used as a border along the base of the house, is typical of Portuguese houses (above). It is often set against a brilliant limewash white or mixed with Yellow or Red Ocher, as seen here.

Mexico

These three Mexican doorways are painted in strong, rich colors that reflect the bright sunlight. The pictures (below left and below center) show how, after years of aging by the sun, layers of paint have resulted in a beautiful patina. The bright pink around the door (below right) is probably a synthetic pigment, but the color originates from the cochineal dye made from an insect found in Mexico and Central and South America.

Egypt
The band of paint at the base of the house (left) is a feature found in many vernacular buildings. It is where the building receives more wear and tear and so needs frequent painting. The Copper Green on the woodwork is one of many shades found in North Africa.

Morocco
In many Mediterranean countries, including Morocco, earth pigments are often mixed into the plaster to give a rich color which ages and patinates well (left). While the walls are drying, they are sometimes rubbed with a rounded pebble to achieve a smooth, polished look.

also known as Persian Red, is a deep purplish red creating maroon-colored paintwork. In Australia, this color is found on the woodwork of early houses, often in combination with dark green, cream, or buff. The same color is also found in France today, from village houses to Parisian bistros. Strong Yellow Ochers are rarely used on woodwork but commonly seen on walls, although pale creams are used, possibly because ocher does not have a lot of tincturing power. All the earth colors have a long history, particularly as wall colors. Depending on the local variations in pigment color and on whether the pigments are mixed into limewash, cooked rye flour paint, or oil, the resulting color can vary from dark brownish reds and mustards to dusty pinks, tawny oranges, and creams.

The second most frequently used group of colors are blues and greens, which were initially based on some form of copper-based pigment. They are nearly always found as a color for woodwork, although there are exceptions, such as the use of Lime Blue in Eastern Europe, Greece, and Portugal. The simplest copper pigment is verdigris, which, although it had a tendency to blacken with age, could be repainted frequently to keep its color. Early production of verdigris centered around Montpelier in France and this may be why

American window
This house (above) has been painted with a Red Oxide-colored paint. The color is often called Barn Red or New England Red, as it is common in that part of the American countryside.

English and Finnish house
The Finnish house (below right) has been painted with classic opaque Finnish cooked paint colored with Yellow Ocher. A similar ocher pigment has been used to color the English house (below), but here the pigment has been mixed with limewash, resulting in a lighter, less intense effect.

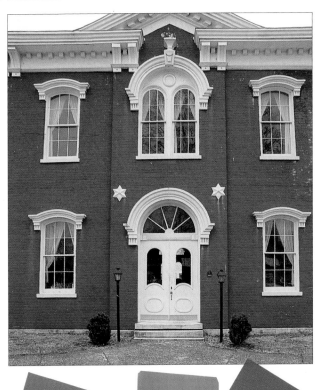

United States
This deep earth red-painted house (above) is reminiscent of houses in Scandinavia, whence immigrants came, possibly bringing their ideas on house painting. This color mixed into a white limewash becomes a soft dusty pink.

Italy
The walls of this Venetian villa (top left) have been painted with a white lime-wash mixed with a local Red Ocher, which makes a soft, earthy, uneven pink. This same color is used in differ-ent shades all over Europe.

France
The woodwork of this French café (right) has been painted a Red Oxide color found all over France. It ranges from a deep velvety maroon-red to a rich chocolate brown.

light and bright blues and greens are still found in this area around the Mediterranean.

In France, clear light blues and a slightly acid light green are found, while in North Africa the greens are more vivid. Darker greens and, to a lesser extent, blues are seen mainly in northern Europe, where a deeper color helps hide the dirt. The greens vary from a yellowish olive to deep, almost black-greens, and blues are often very dark. In the past, unreliable pigments often meant that blue changed to green over a period of time. These colors were also used in Australia and North America at about the same time, as ideas and colors were brought over by the early settlers.

Other color sources, such as plant dyes, have been used in the past. In the north of England, a lichen called archil, and in Scandinavia, the juices of loganberries and blueberries were used to make bluish mauve colors. People continue to be inventive. Today, in Basutoland, Africa, where the inhabitants are poor, old and new methods are combined. The outer and inner walls are covered with different colored clays. Then, mixing powdered pigments with black carbon from old batteries, the women make patterns on the walls.

Recently, there has been more awareness of the importance of paint. In parts of Spain, painting houses with anything other than traditional white limewash is not permitted. All over the world, people are coming to realize that modern colors, such as bright red and lemon yellow, are better placed on modern buildings and older structures are best decorated using a native palette.

Holland
Many houses in Holland are painted a deep, almost black-green (below), with shutter patterns and colors varying according to the region.

Poland
Many houses throughout eastern Europe have been painted like this one in Poland (left), with a wash of Lime Blue, so called because it is a mixture of copper, ammonia, and lime. Nowadays, synthetic Ultramarine offers a cheap alternative.

France

In France, woodwork is often painted in colors which range from the chalky pastel blues and greens (above), found in the south, to the grays and gray-blues found in the north. They are frequently used in combination with a deep reddish brown.

United States

The colors we accept as dating from the Colonial, Federal, and Victorian periods in North America and Australasia tend to reflect the muted tones of popular British colors of the time (right). These may be accurate colors, but it is likely that they faded and became dirty over the years and originally were brighter.

Color Mixing

MOST COMMERCIAL house paints have inspirational names that give no clue to the dyes that color them. It is difficult to predict what sort of color they will produce when they are mixed together. Coloring agents and artist's paints, however, are based on pigments which have remained the same for centuries. They can be used to make paint and to color a glaze or a base with predictable results, depending on the experience of the user. The best way to find out about color mixing is to experiment with a limited range of colors in small proportions and to keep color notes.

Many people know that a green is obtained by mixing blue and yellow, but will have noticed that the result depends on the blues and yellows used. This is because some blues, such as Ultramarine, have red in them and when mixed with a Cadmium Yellow will become a murky green. For a clear green, mix a greenish blue with a greenish yellow.

If a color is very intense and dark, mixing it with a white brings out its characteristics and reveals whether it is warm or cool. If a color is too bright, it can be toned down either with a complementary color or with an earth color such as Raw Umber. The complementary colors are as follows: blue can be darkened with orange, red with green, yellow with purple, and vice versa. Colors are rarely darkened with black as this tends to deaden them.

These pages show a number of key colors which, when mixed with others, provide a wide range of shades. If using acrylic paints or gouache instead of artist's oils, compare the colors on a color chart as they sometimes have different names.

A green-blue
Prussian Blue is an intense greenish blue which appears almost black until it is used with Titanium White or in a dilute form (below).

A bright blue
Cerulean Blue is bright and greenish. With Titanium White it makes a cold pale blue (below). It also makes clear greens with yellow.

A warm gray-blue
Ultramarine is a warm blue. By mixing it with a small amount of Titanium White and Burnt Umber, it becomes a warm gray-blue (below).

A cool gray-blue
Cobalt Blue is a mid-blue with slight green undertones. It has been mixed with Titanium White and Raw Umber to make a cool gray-blue (below).

A warm blue
Ultramarine is the warmest of the blues, and has a hint of crimson in it. It makes a warm pale blue when mixed with Titanium White (above).

Blue and its complementary
Here (right), Ultramarine is mixed with its complementary, Burnt Sienna, and Titanium White, producing a colored gray.

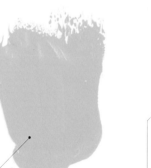

A warm yellow
Cadmium Yellow (above)
is rich and strong. It mixes
well with Cobalt Blue to
create grass and leaf greens.

A dark earth yellow
Raw Sienna and Titanium White
make a warm, neutral, earth color
(above), which is useful for mixing
with a wide range of colors.

Black and white
Black and white together make a
very flat gray (above). Mixed
complementary colors and a white
make grays with added color.

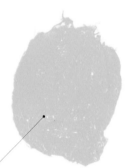

A mid-yellow
Chrome Yellow (above) is
a mid-yellow which will
create richly luminous
oranges and deep yellows.
Mixed with Yellow Ocher,
it makes a bright color.

Yellow and its complementary
The mixed complementary colors of
yellow and purple create neutrals from
brown to black, depending on the
exact colors used (above).

A brown for mixing
Raw Umber has green
undertones, making a
cool, neutral gray when
Titanium White is added
(above). It is good for toning
down hot or bright colors.

A cold yellow
This (above) is
Lemon Yellow, a cold, bright,
slightly greenish color which mixes
well with greenish blues to make
clear greens.

A clear earth yellow
Yellow Ocher is the clearest
of the earth yellows. Mixed
with Red Oxide it makes an
earthy orange (above).

A good black
Ivory black is a
brownish black
with good covering
qualities. It is a
surprisingly warm
color. Titanium
White brings out
its character (left),
which is not clear
until it is diluted.

Green mixed from black
Lemon Yellow and a black mix to a strong olive (below), which can be lightened with the addition of Titanium White.

An earth green
Chromium oxide, a color similar to Earth Green with a slight yellow undertone, makes a quiet but distinctive gray-green when Titanium White is added (above).

A brownish green
Chromium Oxide mixed with Raw Umber makes a dark mossy green (above). Raw Umber is used in place of a black, which tends to deaden color.

Green and its complementary
Here (below) a touch of Cadmium Red (green's complementary color) is added to darken this mid-green. It can be used in varying proportions to alter the degree of brightness.

A mid-green
There is no true mid-green pigment, but some companies make a clear mid-green, like that shown here (right), using a blue and a yellow.

A pale mid-green
Mid-green and Titanium White make a clean, fresh green (above).

A sharp blue
Phthalocyanine Green, Cerulean blue, and Titanium White produce a clean turquoise color (below).

A pale blue-green
Phthalocyanine Green mixed with a little Raw Umber and Titanium White makes a gray, aquamarine color (below).

A muddied green
Phthalocyanine Green and Yellow Ocher produce a muddied green (right).

A cool green
This is a mix of Prussian Blue and Lemon Yellow, making a clear, fresh green (right).

An orange earth red
Burnt Sienna, a rich, warm, earthy red, makes a light orange when mixed with Titanium White (above), and is useful for mixing with blues and greens.

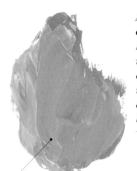

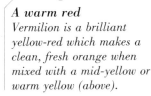

A warm red
Vermilion is a brilliant yellow-red which makes a clean, fresh orange when mixed with a mid-yellow or warm yellow (above).

A mid-earth red
Red Oxide, also called English Red or Light Red, makes a fresh pink when mixed with Titanium White (above).

A rich red
Mixing Cadmium Red and Burnt Umber transforms the red into a warmer, deeper, and richer color (above).

A mid-red
Cadmium Red (above) is a strong, hot mid-red. It is good for mixing warm oranges and browns.

Red and its complementary
Red and green are complementary colors (below), making a range of browns and neutrals when mixed. Adding Titanium White in varying proportions makes a range of warm and cooler neutrals.

A cold red
Alizarin Crimson (below) is a strong blue-red, good for mixing with Ultramarine to make purples and mauves. With Titanium White, it makes baby pink.

A cool earth red
Indian Red is an earth red which shows its plum undertone only when mixed with Titanium White (above).

A cold earth red
Caput Mortuum, meaning "dead head," makes an earthy pale purple when mixed with Titanium White (left).

The House Painter's Techniques

◆ Plaster ◆ Glue and Size ◆
◆ Simple Coatings ◆ Simple Oil Paint ◆
◆ Limewash ◆ Size Paints ◆ Glazes ◆
◆ Casein Paints ◆

ISTORICALLY THERE were two different types of house painting and a distinction should be made between them. High-quality work, found in great and grand houses, was carried out by exceptional, skilled craftsmen using high-quality materials. Farmers, peasants, and workmen, on the other hand, used cheaper, more readily available local materials. They usually made their own paint, passing on their knowledge down the generations. Alternatively, they employed traveling craftsmen who got free board and lodging in exchange for some work.

Paint was made from local materials, such as lime and chalk, which made cheap and effective paints. Lime is a disinfectant and both walls and woodwork were painted with it as part of the annual spring-cleaning; it was also used on stables and outbuildings. Chalk was dug from local pits and added to glue made from animal bones and hide. Chalk was used to make a paint called calcimine/distemper, frequently applied to walls and ceilings in grander houses.

Other ingredients, such as milk, oats, and eggs, were used to make paint. These paints were often colored with local earth pigments. In America, a milk paint bound with lime was used by the early settlers, who also adapted stranger methods of making paint, such as using salmon eggs, from Native Americans.

From the 1600s onward, both the owners of grand houses in Europe and artisans became preoccupied with the art of painting interiors with pigments ground in oil. Domestic architecture underwent great changes. Houses and palaces with magnificent interiors were being designed, as well as houses on a more modest scale. The ceilings were still painted with the traditional calcimine/distemper, but the walls were often paneled with wood and painted with oil paint. Other wall coverings at this time included flock papers, Oriental, hand-painted bird and flower papers,

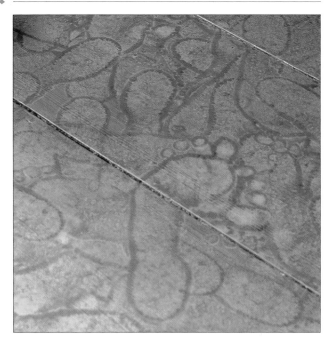

The house painter, especially in rural areas, used to be proficient in more than just plain painting. This floor (above) is decorated with a technique typical of floors in Holland. First, a light color is applied. When it is dry, a darker color oil glaze is painted over the surface. While the glaze is still wet, people, particularly children, walk across it in their bare feet, leaving an interesting pattern of spots and ovals.

damasks, and velvets, as well as painted canvas wall hangings.

Oil paint was made with different types of oil according to availability and region. In 18th- and 19th-century France, poppy oil was used (from the opium, not the Flanders poppy). In England, linseed oil was common and the longer-lasting walnut oil was used for quality work. Traditional oil paint is a mixture of raw linseed oil, pigment, a thinning solvent (turpentine being the earliest and, for years, the only solvent used), and driers. Paint makers refined the linseed oil and added mastic

These two brushes (left) have changed little over the years. The large one, which is made of vegetable fiber, is lime-resistant, so it is used for limewashing. The small bristle brush is a typical European design used for oil painting.

This Irish house (left) has always been whitewashed or limewashed each year before the Feast of Corpus Christi. This was the traditional date by which all spring-cleaning was finished.

Stockholm tar (opposite), a type of wood tar, was used as a protective layer on houses in Scandinavia, Germany, and Holland, replacing the pig's fat that was previously used.

resin to produce higher gloss. The blend, sometimes called Megilp, of resin and oil made a paint known as "hard gloss paint."

The training of professional painters was in the hands of a craftsman's guild. House painters were referred to as broad brush painters or coarse painters, as opposed to fine artists who painted pictures using finer brushes. Coarse painters included the replication of marbles and woods, among many other skills, in their repertoires.

The painter and decorator made his own paint in his workshop by grinding pigments and mixing the basic ingredients. The pigment was ground using a muller and grinding stone. It was then placed on a marble slab and mixed together with linseed oil using a palette knife until thoroughly combined. This was a laborious method of making paint and only a relatively small amount could be mixed in this way, but paint was valuable and the painter used very small quantities.

By the late 18th century, the demand for all types of paint had increased to such an extent that it became worthwhile to manufacture paint for other people to use. There are records of paint made with white lead and Prussian Blue ground into oil by laborious manual work or by the use of a horse mill. In 1769, John Gore of Boston advertised "very good red, black, yellow paints, the produce and manufacture of North America." Nevertheless, it was not until the 1920s that ready-made paints came into common use.

Hopper mills appeared in the middle of the 19th century. They could mill 55 lb/25 kg of paint a day

and remained in use until the beginning of the 20th century. The fineness of the paint was determined by the number of times it was put through the mill. This job would have been done by the youngest apprentice. The mysteries of the ground pigment, the medium, and various additives to help drying were set out in a wide variety of manuals with extensive directions and methods.

During this period and for centuries before, white lead formed the principal basis of many colors, as titanium oxide does today. The ancient Greeks made white lead by a process called the "stack process." Ordinary lead was sealed in clay

Holding the paint brush as shown (left) and painting in a criss-cross manner ensures that the paint is brushed out thoroughly and evenly.

pots with a weak solution of vinegar. The pots were stacked, separated with dung or tanner's bark to provide carbon dioxide and warmth, and left for about three months. The vinegar vapor and fermenting bark converted the lead to white lead.

In 16th-century England, red lead pigment was made by heating white lead, which turned yellow-orange and then red. The paint was called "lethargе" because of the symptoms of the workers who suffered from lead poisoning. Red lead was used as a primer and as a pigment.

Paint is now ground with steel rollers and the coloring matter is so fine that it becomes a dye rather than a pigment. This is why modern paints are so uniform in color. Classic paints made by craftsmen were often uneven in the way they were applied, and the pigments were sometimes crudely ground so that they stood out. The resulting effect was very different from the flat/mat paints commonly available today.

Plaster

PINK, FRESHLY plastered walls and other decorated plaster treatments find their original inspiration in the painted murals of Italy and the Mediterranean, where sun and rain have weathered the ocher or bright blue walls.

Classic plaster walls were and are made from lime and sand. Often, a coarser layer that included a binding of horsehair or some similar material was used before a final, fine, smooth layer was applied. Classic lime plaster is particularly suitable for houses which have been built without a damp course (an impervious layer inserted into brick walls to prevent damp rising), as it allows for natural evaporation. These walls should be painted with limewash or calcimine/distemper; both are permeable and will not blister or peel.

Modern plasters are available in two finishes; a bonding and a finishing coat. Freshly plastered walls that are going to be sealed with wax or varnish or decorated with a non-porous treatment, such as a modern latex/vinyl emulsion paint, should be allowed to dry out for a minimum of six weeks; moisture continues to evaporate from them for up to six months. The longer they are left to dry out, the better. It has been estimated that the plastered interior surfaces in a newly built house of average size contain more than one ton of water. Sealing such surfaces with wax, varnish, or a non-porous paint invites trouble.

A new plaster wall is extremely absorbent and should be sized or primed with thin paint, polyvinyl acrylic/PVA, or size. A solution of equal parts water and polyvinyl acrylic/PVA is easy to prepare and apply, and quick drying. Alternatively, a solution of rabbitskin glue size or very thin paint may be used as a primer. The primer may be a thinned-down version of the coating with which the surface will eventually be treated.

Materials and equipment

These are the materials used to create the effects on the following plaster samples although many other materials could be used. The effects on plaster are endless. Begin by experimenting on small surface areas.

Clear proprietary wax

Bronze powder

Elm-colored wax

Pearl luster powder

Clear beeswax

Mars Violet

Red Ocher

Large brush

Ultramarine

Raw Umber

Natural linseed oil glaze

Fine grade steelwool

Polyvinyl acrylic/PVA

Cloth for applying bronze powder

Casein glue, Mars Violet and Titanium White paint mixture

Plaster is available in various colors; pale and darker pink, white, and gray are the most usual. These can be smoothed off with a finish plaster (a final, very fine coat). It is also possible to add pigment to the plaster before it is applied for a more durable, bound-in color.

Plaster does not have to be flat and smooth. It can have a rough, undulating surface reminiscent of that found in old country cottages. To obtain such a surface, either the finishing coat can be omitted or a coarse sand and mortar mixture can be applied using a plaster trowel/wooden float.

If you are lucky enough to have the old lime plaster walls once so common in Europe and North America, you should carefully restore and preserve them. If you have other types of old walls then you can make a virtue of them by color washing. This is traditionally done with oil glaze over a simple oil paint for walls (eggshell is now normally used in place of the latter). The paint can be distressed using a wide brush or rags. While the paint is still slightly tacky, wipe over the surface with a clean rag. This will remove the paint from the highest points only. Do this in a "carefully careless" way.

The advantages of many of the techniques shown here are that they can be cheap, quick, simple to apply, and flexible, depending on the state of the wall. Colors and treatments can be easily washed over in order to change color, depth of color, or sheen. A quick and easy method is to mix thin washes in a bucket and apply them with large cotton cloths or sponges. Large brushes, such as wallpaper brushes and ordinary household paint brushes, may be used. Techniques can be tried and

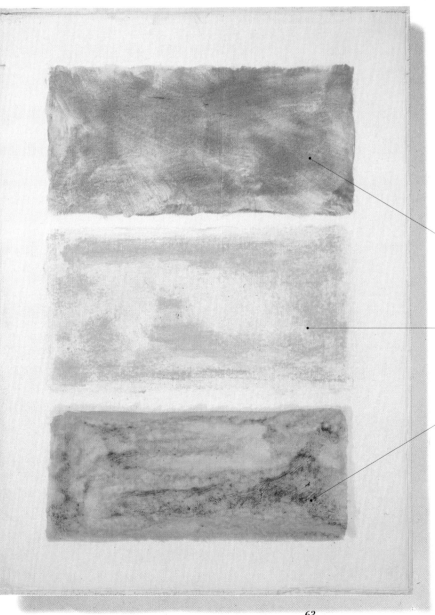

Gray plaster
This plaster (left) is the coolest of the plaster colors and so a blue/gray color range seems to be the natural choice. It could be warmed up by painting a thin wash of Indian Red pigment over it.

Ultramarine
Ultramarine pigment and linseed oil glaze were brushed on with water (top left).

Clear wax
Gray plaster was covered with a proprietary, plain, uncolored wax (center left).

Polyvinyl acrylic/PVA
This is a wash of polyvinyl acrylic/PVA over gray plaster (bottom left).

then wiped off before the paint is dry if they do not work. Colors can then be rubbed back with blocks of wet and dry or dry sandpaper. This process works surprisingly quickly, even on a large wall. Colors can be altered by covering them with a glaze made from transparent oil glaze, turpentine, and artist's oil paint, or polyvinyl acrylic/PVA and acrylics, or acrylic glaze and water-based paint. Washes can be made with pigment and water as long as they are sealed with varnish afterwards to prevent the pigment from rubbing off.

If polyvinyl acrylic/PVA is used in the mixture, the durability of the surface is dependent upon the proportions. The higher the proportion of polyvinyl acrylic/PVA, the more waterproof the surface will be. For instance, a small amount of polyvinyl acrylic/PVA will make the coat resistant to touch but not to water. This is not suitable for bathrooms

therefore, but this characteristic could be viewed as an advantage since the old coat can be washed off and replaced with a new color very easily. If a more permanent coating is required, an acrylic varnish could be colored and then washed over the wall. Some of the waxes shown here are soft and so not suitable for every situation. Other sealants, such as shellac and varnishes, may also be used.

Sgraffito
This (above) is a fresco technique. The pigment is mixed with the mortar in the final layer. Lime putty is painted on the surface and when the surface is almost dry, it is scratched back to reveal the colored layer.

Pale pink plaster
This plaster (left) is a pleasant warm color in itself and so looks good with just a transparent seal. It is also light enough to provide a background for a whole variety of other colors.

Clear beeswax
A clear beeswax was rubbed on and then rubbed back with both a cotton cloth and steelwool (top left).

Elm-colored wax
A proprietary wax, which contains a color to imitate elmwood, was rubbed in and later polished (center left).

Red Ocher pigment
Red Ocher pigment, polyvinyl acrylic/ PVA, and water were brushed over untreated plaster (bottom left).

White plaster
The most adaptable of the four basic plaster colors, it (left) can also be tinted before being applied by adding some pigment to the plaster powder.

Bronze powder
Polyvinyl acrylic/PVA was painted on and allowed to dry until tacky. Bronze powder was applied with a soft cotton cloth and partly rubbed in (top left).

Mars Violet and a white
Casein glue, Mars Violet, and Titanium White were mixed with water (not more than 50 per cent) and lightly sanded back with the finest grade sandpaper (center left).

Mars Violet
A wash of Mars Violet was brushed on over unsealed plaster (bottom left).

Pink plaster
The darkest of the plasters, this (right) is also the warmest in tone and contrasts well with blue paintwork.

Pearl luster powder
Pearl luster was applied over unsealed plaster and polyvinyl acrylic/PVA (top right).

Raw Umber
Unsealed plaster was scratched back with a metal bristled brush. Raw Umber and water were rubbed in with a cloth. The plaster was rubbed back again with the brush and steelwool (center right).

Polyvinyl acrylic/PVA
Plain pink plaster has been sealed with polyvinyl acrylic/PVA (bottom right).

Glue and Size

SIZE, SOMETIMES known as glue size, has two main functions: as a medium to bind paint, such as soft calcimine/distemper, and as a sealant to reduce the absorbency of a surface before it is painted. Because of its adaptability, it was once an important material in the house painter's workshop, but it has now been largely replaced by primers and manufactured paints.

Primers and sizes are both used to prepare surfaces for painting. The difference between them is that a primer is a paint and, therefore, opaque, while a size is transparent. If a surface is not sealed before painting, it will absorb too much paint, which is uneconomical. It is important to use a size or primer sympathetic to the type of paint that is going to be applied over it. Therefore, a plastic-based size, such as polyvinyl acrylic/PVA, works well with modern latex paints/vinyl emulsions. A decorator using soft calcimine/distemper, a paint made from whiting and glue size, would seal the walls first with a thinned glue size, which would also act as a bond between the wall and the paint, ensuring lasting adhesion. Another example of this bonding is when a new plaster wall is sized with a thin coat of wallpaper paste before the wallpaper is hung. Both fresh plaster and untreated wood have a high rate of absorbency and must be sized.

Classic sizes are all animal in origin. The most frequently used is made with animal skin and bones. Rabbitskin glue size is the most easily available, and is particularly popular in the gilding trade as it is an essential ingredient of gesso (*see pages 90–93*). Calfskin glue is like rabbitskin glue, but less flexible and not so readily available.

Polyvinyl acrylic/PVA
Polyvinyl acrylic/PVA (right) is a modern, highly adaptable glue. It can be used as a binder for paint and glaze as well as a size. It is white in appearance but dries to a shiny transparency. It is also used instead of polymer resins in the manufacture of a cheap range of children's paints.

Isinglass
Fish have often been used as a source for cold glues. While not as durable or effective as animal bone or skin glues, fish glues can be used cold, which is an advantage. The best sort, isinglass (above left), is made from the swim bladder of the sturgeon. It is expensive and mainly used for special purposes, such as gilding.

Casein glue
This (above) is pure lactic casein glue for emulsions and for binding pigments. It may also be used to size wood before decorating with casein paints.

Pearl glue
This cheap animal glue (above left) is called pearl glue after its appearance. It is also known as Scotch glue. Soak for 3 hours before use.

Making size requires time. It can be bought in granules or sheet form, but it is more difficult to measure accurate proportions with the latter. Size is soaked in cold water in order to fatten up – the granules become swollen – and then more water is added. The usual proportions are one part glue size to 20 parts of water in total. Heat the size until the granules melt and a sticky liquid forms. If animal size is allowed to boil, it becomes brittle.

Although most sizes need heat to melt them, some, such as those made from fish, isinglass for example, do not. Those that do need heating have to be used while still warm, otherwise they revert to a gel. Animal size can be kept in the refrigerator for up to a week before it goes bad, but it thickens on standing and adding water weakens it.

The type of size you should use depends greatly on the application. Higher quality and more expensive sizes, such as leaf gelatin, are generally used for fine work as they provide a smoother, thinner finish, and are almost completely transparent. The commoner and less refined animal glue sizes are all slightly colored and are used for more robust work such as for the sizing of walls or for using in calcimines/distempers.

Sizes and polyvinyl acrylic/PVA mediums can also be used as glues, indeed size is itself simply a refined type of glue. The modern equivalent of size is polymer vinyl mediums which are generally sold as glue for crafts. These do not have the flexibility of traditional glue size and they are not made from natural materials.

Parchment clippings
Parchment clippings (right) are made from the skin of a sheep's neck. They are boiled slowly in water for four to six hours. It was once thought to be the best glue for making distemper.

Rabbitskin gel
When glue size or gelatin is soaked overnight and then heated, it makes a gel (below). This solidifies on cooling. It can be rendered back to glue by reheating.

Leaf gelatin
Gelatin (above) is a good size for very delicate work. It is made from bones, but is more refined and less colored than ordinary bone glue. Soak 6 leaves in 2½ cups/600 ml/20 fl oz water for 15 minutes until the gelatin swells. Then heat in a double boiler until it dissolves. Leave to cool but do not allow it to set.

Rabbitskin granules
Rabbitskin glue is sold in thin squares or as coarse or finer granules (above right). It has a relatively dark color and is very flexible. It is used for many decorative purposes, such as the manufacture of gesso and paints. Hide glue, made from cowskin, is also available. It looks very similar but is not as flexible as rabbitskin glue.

Simple Coatings

NTIL THE mid-1800s, when factories began to manufacture paint, it was either made from its basic ingredients at home or by itinerant craftsmen. As prehistoric peoples discovered, and as decorators have been discovering ever since, paint can be made with anything that sticks onto a surface.

The sticky matter in paint is called the vehicle, medium, or binder. The most successful binders are transparent, stick to the substrate, and dry within a reasonable period of time. Furthermore, a good paint is long lasting and neither flakes nor cracks. Many old paints were made with curious binders. Pliny mentions milk and egg being used in ancient wall paintings, substances both still used by painters today. Odder constituents included beer (still used for woodgraining), vinegar, wine, and the milky juices of the fig tree. Not many of these materials make a strong, durable paint on their own. Throughout history, painters have been trying out different combinations in the search for a better, longer-lasting paint.

Paint was made with whatever ingredients were readily available. In America, homesteaders copied the Indians who used salmon eggs and red cedar bark. Presumably, cedar wood produced a resin and salmon eggs were sticky.

Early paint is not well documented. Recipes passed from father to son by word of mouth. Medieval painters formed themselves into guilds and encouraged secrecy so as to safeguard their members and their skills. It was not until the 17th century that any information about house paints first appeared in books.

There was a difference between quality paintwork and paintwork on the farm. Country people used the materials on hand, such as milk, oats, and

MAKING MILK PAINT

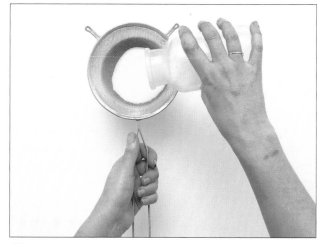

1 Pour the sour milk through a strainer into a bowl to separate the curds and whey. Alternatively, strain it through cheesecloth.

Simple milk paint
A very simple paint may be made from sour skim milk (left). The milk should be left in a warm atmosphere until it separates. Here (below) simple milk paint colored with Chrome Green pigment has been applied to a plaster surface where it has remained unchanged for two years. Surprisingly, perhaps, many modern paints, developed with all the advantages of 20th-century technology, do not last so long as traditional homemade paints.

eggs, as well as chalk and lime from the earth. A paint is still produced in Finland which is identical to one made centuries ago. It is a kind of calcimine/distemper which uses a starch base as a binder. There are records of its use in the Middle Ages, although the present recipe dates from the 1750s. It is made with a vegetable glue produced by boiling wheat flour for several hours. Like calcimine/distemper, which is made with animal glue size, it allows the surface to ''breathe.'' This type of paint can last up to 30 years, considerably longer than modern paints, because it does not flake off but gradually wears away.

It is important to recognize that homemade paint is still rather unpredictable. For the last few decades manufacturers have concentrated on producing paints which are uniform in color and surface texture. We have come to expect a certain predictability about the paint that we buy.

The simplest way of making paint at home is with skim milk. Leave it to turn sour; bacteria promote the formation of lactic acid which will precipitate casein. Casein is a protein in milk and forms the binder of the paint. When the milk has turned sour, it separates into curds and whey. The whey can be poured off and the thick curds made into paint by the addition of pigment. Milk paint made simply from curds can have a biocidal added to prevent mold growth. You can use a few drops of oil of cloves or oil of spike lavender. This is a very simple paint which is cheap and easy to make. It is still used in certain remote country areas, particularly on exterior walls.

The binding power of skim milk is low because it contains only a small proportion of casein. Longer-lasting and more substantial milk or casein paints are made commercially for artists and house painters by adding lime, ammonia, or borax.

2 *Transfer the curds to a bowl. They will look a little like yoghurt and may be slightly lumpy.*

3 *Add a small amount of pigment, in this case Chrome Green, and stir thoroughly to disperse it. Continue adding pigment until the desired shade is reached.*

Simple Oil Paint

Until the 20th century, paint was made from materials that were mostly vegetable in origin, apart from lead and the mineral content of some pigments. Classic paints have a completely different texture from contemporary paints. The old paints sank into the wood, whereas our modern paints make a film which eventually cracks and peels.

Most of the protective coatings of the past came from locally available materials. In the 16th century, wooden buildings in Holland were protected with pig fat which made the wood a yellow color. The fat was melted over glowing peat and then brushed on with huge brushes. Whale blubber and, later on, a Swedish tar, known as Stockholm tar, were used to protect the exterior of wooden buildings, particularly in Northern Europe.

A paint can be made with any vegetable oil as long as it is a drying oil, but linseed oil is the most widely used. Olive oil, for example, is not suitable as it will not dry. Linseed oil was refined and natural resin was added to make the paint spread better, dry quicker, and give a higher gloss. In the 18th and 19th centuries, the French used the oil of the opium poppy, the English, linseed oil for general work and the longer-lasting walnut oil for quality work, and the Americans used peanut oil.

The blend of resin and oil became known as varnish, and paint made with this as a medium became known as varnish paint, and, later, as "hard gloss paint."

To produce linseed oil, the flax seeds are ground under stones, heated, and the oil pressed out using great force. This produces raw linseed oil, which "ripens"

and is ready for use as a binder after three months. The qualities of linseed oil can be improved by bleaching or boiling. It then dries more quickly and is more durable. Stand oil, linseed oil that has been heated to 572° F/300° C, has a high gloss, and is even more durable.

A very simple oil paint can be made using just linseed oil, turpentine, and pigment. The paint shown here was made using boiled linseed oil as a drying medium. While making the paint, the mixture must be stirred constantly so that the pigment is absorbed. This process used to be done on a large scale with a cannon ball rolling around a large kettle hung on chains. The paint is made into a flowing medium by the addition of raw linseed oil, and then into a flowing paint with turpentine. The final consistency is that of chocolate sauce. Test the consistency by brushing it out. If the paint makes ridges or ropes, it needs more turpentine. The paint should be sufficiently thin without falling. Several coats are better than one and it is better to apply alternate fat (oil-rich) and thin layers. Finally the paint must be strained; if it is gritty, it will lose its flow and viscosity.

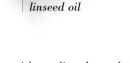

Mixing bowl with wooden spoon

Raw linseed oil

Turpentine

Boiled linseed oil

Red Ocher pigment

Paint can with muslin, cheesecloth, stockinette or old pantyhose used as a strainer

Materials and equipment
No specialist materials or equipment are required to make this paint. Some pigments absorb more oil than others, particularly the oxides, which have a drying effect on the oil. For this reason it is impossible to give precise measures for mixing. Start with about 1 part pigment to 1 part boiled linseed oil and adjust according to the pigment and the strength of color required.

MIXING SIMPLE OIL PAINT

1 *Pour the boiled linseed oil into a glass bowl. Swirl the bowl around so that the sides of the bowl are coated.*

2 *Add the pigment and more boiled linseed oil. Stir to a paste. Blend it like a cake mix, until it forms a heavy dough and drops very slowly off the spoon.*

3 *Keep stirring so that all the pigment is absorbed into the boiled linseed oil. Add enough raw linseed oil to make a flowing medium.*

4 *Add the turpentine until the paint has the consistency of chocolate sauce. Test the consistency of the paint by brushing out a sample.*

5 *Strain the mixture through muslin, cheesecloth or old pantyhose into a paint can, pushing it through with the wooden spoon.*

6 *When applying, use a well-worked brush, working in every direction around the compass. Lay it off with a new brush, either with or against the grain.*

Limewash

LIMEWASH IS A classic, durable coating that lets the wall "breathe;" it allows for the passage of moisture. Most houses and buildings in North America, Europe, and Australasia used to be limewashed once a year. The leftovers in the bucket were used to disinfect and protect the furniture; liming wax is now used (*see pages 120–121*). Lime can be bought in a dry form or ready-slaked (combined with water) as lime putty.

Limewash is a coating used as a protective, decorative paint in many countries. It works in harmony with the buildings, the environment, and the people who live with it. In Spain there are even conservation areas where, by law, houses must be painted with white limewash so as to retain the character of the local environment. Limewash also has a soft, mat quality pleasing to the touch, and, contrary to some opinions, if it has been properly mixed, does not come off when brushed against.

Houses built without a damp course, an impervious layer inserted into brick walls to prevent damp rising, benefit from coating with limewash, as the moisture in the wall is allowed to evaporate rather than having to break through a sealed surface. Most modern coatings, such as latex/vinyl emulsions, are plastic paints which form a seal over the wall rather than soaking into the surface. This is why modern paint blisters and cracks; a coating like limewash will mature and mellow with age, and moves closely with the structure of the building. It can help to strengthen and improve old walls, and the alkali acts as a disinfectant.

One of its few disadvantages is that limewash cannot be painted over modern emulsions, as it needs to sink into a permeable surface, such as lime plaster, brick, or existing limewash. In addition, lime is caustic when wet, so it needs to be handled carefully. It is a good idea to clear the area completely before you start painting to avoid accidents, and to take sensible precautions if you are not used to handling it. It is important to protect the floor with an old cloth or strong plastic sheeting and

Traditional country kitchen
This cottage kitchen (opposite) is a typical example of where limewash should be used. The house was built on different levels and the back wall of the kitchen was dug out of the earth. The green limewash (left) provides a beautifully modulated textured color, and protects and preserves the fabric of the building.

to wear protective clothing. You may also wish to wear protective goggles in case of splashback.

Without the addition of pigment, limewash remains white – the color of the lime – but any pigment can be added to color it. Limewash can also be combined with other ingredients. In North America it is mixed with casein to make what is often known as milk paint or buttermilk paint.

The following pages explain how to slake lime, that is, adding water to lime to make lime putty, and how to make a limewash and apply it to a wall. Our example shows an exterior wall which has previously been limewashed, but the same lime-wash could have been applied to an interior wall which had been lime plastered or gypsum plas-tered. It is possible to apply limewash over latex/vinyl emulsion if the paint has been rubbed down to make the surface more porous. However, it will lie on the surface rather than be absorbed. It defeats the object of using a paint that "breathes" to apply it over a plastic paint. The tools and materials for limewashing, with the exception of the lime, are easily obtainable. Lime must be bought from a specialty supplier. Slaked lime can be bought ready-prepared, and simply needs water added to make the right consistency. During its preparation, lime is heated, occasionally unevenly, so that some lumps take longer to slake than others.

A short bristle brush is best for applying lime-wash as the wash is runnier than paint and tends to splash. Short bristle brushes work better at pushing the limewash into the wall. When pigment is added to the limewash, it dries to a much mellower color than the original color in the bucket. You may wish to test a color swatch with the pigmented limewash before covering the entire surface. Remember, the pigmented wash will also tend to mature with the passage of time. (*See page 129 for a list of lime-proof pigments.*)

Materials and equipment

The basic equipment is inexpensive and easy to obtain, but it is important to have adequate protection for yourself and the surrounding area. Lime can be bought from specialty sup-pliers around the country. Do not confuse quick lime with builder's lime (hydrated lime), which also comes in dry form.

Protective gloves and goggles

Mixing tool or kitchen whisk

Short bristle brush

Measuring cup

Quick lime

Cup for mixing pigment

Pigment

Kitchen strainer

Bucket for mixing limewash

Bucket for mixing lime putty

MAKING LIME PUTTY AND LIMEWASH

1 *Protect your hands with rubber gloves. To slake the lime, first pour warm water into a builder's bucket. You will need ½ gallon/2 liters of warm water to about 4 handfuls of lime.*

2 *Add the lime to the water. The mixture will hiss, bubble, and release heat and steam. The steam is not dangerous, but it is advisable not to breathe it in.*

3 *Stir with a mixing tool or old kitchen whisk until all the lumps have been dissolved completely. Once the slaking reaction has stopped, add water until a good working consistency is reached.*

4 *Pass the lime through a strainer to remove any unslaked lumps. Because lime is sometimes heated unevenly during its preparation, some lumps take longer to slake than others.*

5 *If you are using a color, mix the pigment with a small amount of water in a cup. When the powder has dissolved, add it to the lime putty or limewash. Lime dries to a slightly lighter shade.*

Traditional color

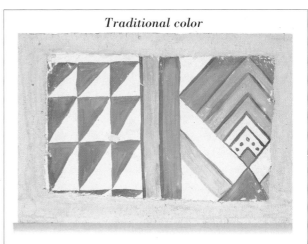

This is part of a wall decoration painted with colored limewash onto a white limewashed wall (above). This was a very early method of wall decoration.

APPLYING LIMEWASH TO A WALL

1 Brush down the wall with a stiff bristle brush to remove any dust and loose particles. The wall should be porous, that is, plaster, brick, or previously limewashed.

2 Splash the wall with clean water and brush over the surface evenly. This reduces the absorbency of the wall, thus limiting the rate at which the limewash dries out.

3 Using a short bristle brush, apply the limewash evenly onto the wall, brushing it in well.

4 This portion of the wall shows the texture of the limewash and the difference in color and appearance between the wet and the dry limewash.

Creating a mood
*The walls of this tiny blue bathroom vibrate with color to
make a welcoming room. The feel and look of the limewash is smooth, soft, and soothing.*

Size Paints

SIZE PAINTS are very simple paints of which the best known is calcimine/distemper. It was often used for less important parts of the house as it was cheap and easily applied. It was only superseded when commercial latex/vinyl emulsion paints were developed. Calcimine/distemper is now used by architectural conservationists and home decorators who are interested in authenticity and environmental concerns. Made from natural materials, it gives a smooth, flat/mat finish and comes in two types: soft and oil-bound.

Soft calcimine/distemper is made from a mixture of whiting and water to which a glue size is added. On cooling, it becomes a thin gel which is then brushed on. It is particularly suitable for use on molded plaster, such as cornices and ceiling roses, as it can be washed off before repainting so there is no build-up of paint. Repeated applications of modern paints, however, fill in and obscure such intricate details.

The advantages of using calcimine/distemper rather than a modern paint are the velvety, smooth

MAKING SOFT CALCIMINE/DISTEMPER

1 Add 7¾ lb/3.5 kg whiting to a bucket of water, whisking to remove the lumps. Set it aside so that the whiting sinks to the bottom.

2 Pour 2½ cups/600 ml hot water onto 4 oz/113 g concentrated calfskin size granules. Set aside to soak for at least 3 hours and preferably overnight to fatten up.

3 Thoroughly whisk the size mixture and heat in a double boiler to make it liquid.

4 Carefully pour off the surplus water from the whiting. The longer the whiting is left to fatten up the better.

Materials and equipment

Use a fine grade of whiting but not as fine as gesso whiting or the mixture will become a paste. Use calfskin glue, which is less flexible than rabbitskin.

Glue size

Ultramarine pigment

Whiting

Whisk

Teaspoon

Calcimine/ distemper brush

Measuring cup

Paint can

Strainer and bucket

5 *Add 1 level teaspoon Ultramarine pigment to the whiting and whisk it in. This will counteract the color of the size and whiten the calcimine/distemper.*

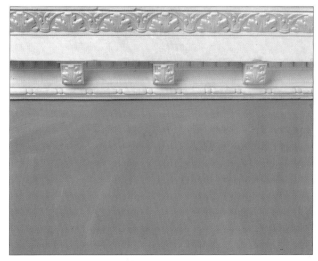

6 *Pour the heated glue into the whiting through a strainer. Whisk it into the whiting. The calcimine/ distemper will turn into a thick gel on cooling.*

7 *Pigment may be added to color the calcimine/ distemper. Whisk to disperse the powder. Make a test swatch; wet paint will be darker than dry color.*

8 *It is traditional to paint the ceiling and the cornices white and to add color to the wall coating.*

texture and the quality of the finished surface. It also has the advantage of being permeable, allowing the wall to "breathe," unlike modern paints which coat walls with a plastic film. It looks slightly chalky, has no shine, and yet avoids a dull, lifeless look. This is partly because pigments are used rather than dyes as in modern paints. The color is therefore intense, even in the palest tones.

When making up calcimine/distemper, test it by painting a piece of white paper. If it has too much glue, it will crack off when dry, that is, it is overbound. If it does not have enough, it will powder. People often associate calcimine/distemper with flaking or powdery walls, but if it is made properly, using the correct proportions of whiting to glue size, it will not come off when brushed against. In the past, decorators often deliberately used insufficient size – thereby keeping the solution weak – as they were not paid if the paint cracked off. When the glue size and whiting mixture has cooled, the paint becomes a weak, trembling gel. As the glue is an animal product, wet calcimine/distemper will spoil if it is kept for too long. Philatol or carbolic acid will help preserve it. It should be kept in a cool place and used within a week (four weeks if a bicodil is used).

Surfaces should be sized with glue size before calcimine/distemper is applied, otherwise the plaster will suck the paint into the wall. It is a one-coat material so the paint edge has to be kept wet as you work. If the edge dries and the coating is overlapped, the edge will appear darker. Apply the paint in straight lines. Make sure that there are no draughts about while you are working. Open windows and doors when the room is finished.

When making calcimine/distemper, you should add the pigment before the glue cools. Dilute the pigment first with a little water for an even color. Traditionally the pigment was added straight to the whiting and glue size mixture. This tends to produce a more exciting effect as small areas of stronger color will appear.

The disadvantage of painting with calcimine/distemper is that it cannot be used to cover modern paints; only calcimine/distemper should be used to cover calcimine/distemper. Both oil-bound and soft calcimine/distemper are best applied to bare plaster, lime plaster, or a surface which has previously been treated with a similar coating. It may be possible to apply calcimine/distemper to a surface which has been painted with some other kind of paint, but it will not be so durable and in some instances, may not take at all. The only way to find out is to experiment. A new plaster wall should be treated with a thin coating unless the instructions on the paint can specify otherwise. The covering power of soft calcimine/distemper is about the same as a solid latex/vinyl emulsion paint.

Soft calcimine/distemper can be used only for internal walls, while oil-bound calcimine/distemper is suitable for both internal and external work as the addition of oil makes it stronger. Unlike soft calcimine/distemper, oil-bound calcimine/distemper is only obtainable ready-made.

Traditional effect
This wall (left) has been painted in oil-bound calcimine/distemper. It may be wiped clean, but cannot be scrubbed.

Oil-bound calcimine/distemper
Oil-bound calcimine/distemper (opposite) is suitable for walls which may need washing – in halls, kitchens, or bathrooms – but it is not as tough as modern plastic paints. Oil-bound calcimine/distemper for external use contains binders to make it scrubbable and able to withstand inclement weather.

Glazes

A GLAZE IS A transparent coat of paint that is thinly brushed out over a basecoat. It consists of a small amount of pigment suspended in a clear medium. It should not be confused with a thin wash of paint, which is usually opaque. Classic glazes are either water-based, with beer as a medium, or oil-based, with linseed oil as a medium. Acrylic glazes are a recent innovation. Proprietary brands of glaze are available in cans, but you can make your own using linseed oil, turpentine, and driers.

Glazes are painted over basecoats to create various decorative effects. Nowadays, an oil-based eggshell paint is used for the basecoat. In many decorative techniques, the glaze is brushed on thinly over the dry basecoat and then partially lifted off with specialty brushes. As the glaze is transparent, it reveals the underlying basecoat to create an illusion of depth. Several glaze coats can be built up in layers to achieve a color of astonishing brilliance and depth.

Glaze coats were originally called "flatting" coats, and were used over oil paint on the interior walls of fine houses, particularly on wood paneling. The oil paint was absorbed into the paneling unevenly, so a flatting coat was applied to improve its appearance. It was probably painted over a basecoat that was dry but not completely hardened, so that the flatting coat slightly dissolved and was absorbed into the surface. Initially, the flatting coat was made of turpentine and pigment.

In recent years, modern tastes have developed oil-glaze techniques into a creative and lively section of the decorative arts, used on furniture, walls, and woodwork. Many of these techniques, which we know today by such names as ragging and strié/dragging, are directly related to woodgraining and imitating marble (*faux marbre*).

Woodgraining was a popular 18th- and 19th-century paint finish. Cheap woods were painted to imitate more expensive and exotic varieties which had to be imported and were difficult to obtain. It was developed into a highly skilled art, where the painted wood was virtually indistinguishable from the real thing. The most commonly imitated woods were birdseye maple, oak, satinwood, mahogany, walnut, and rosewood.

Marbling has always been done by painting oil glaze over an oil-based ground. It was a mixture of glazing and scumbling. The most popular marbles were white-veined, Florentine, black and gold, Egyptian porphyry, Sienna, and St. Remi marble. The first coat was smooth as possible and a coat of varnish at the end provided the high gloss finish.

Glaze is also used in decorative techniques which imitate precious or semiprecious stones and other materials, such as malachite, lapis lazuli, and tortoiseshell.

Acrylic water glaze

Siccative

Linseed oil

Scumble glaze

Scumble glaze
Despite its yellowish color, scumble glaze (right) is transparent when diluted by half with turpentine and applied thinly. There are various makes, each with its own particular quality. In recent years, acrylic water glazes (right) have become available. While quicker-drying than oil scumbles, they dry more slowly than the traditional water glazes (right).

Beer
Because of its stickiness, beer (above) is used in water glazes to carry the pigment over an oil background. Sometimes honey is used.

Linseed oil and water glaze

A homemade oil glaze
A homemade oil glaze can be made using boiled linseed oil (above), with an equal quantity of turpentine and a little drier or siccative (above left). Color, in the form of either stainers, oil color, or dry pigment, is then added.

Woodgraining
Craftsmen in the 19th century became expert at graining in intricate patterns to suggest inlay and marquetry. These large double doors were painted by the 19th-century Bolton grainer, Thomas Kershaw (1819–98). The flowers in the central panels are hand painted.

Casein Paints

CASEIN IS A protein that acts as a binder. It has proved invaluable as a medium for painters and can be used in a variety of ways: to make a ground for overpainting, or gilding, to make a glue or a size, or as a binder for paint. Casein has been used since earliest recorded times, in *secco* painting in fresco, and by farmers for painting simple furniture.

There are many different recipes for making casein paints, but the casein itself is manufactured from sour skim milk. The curd is separated from the whey, washed, and then dried. It is possible to make a form of simple paint from the curds alone (*see pages 68–69*), but it is not very permanent. Commercial manufacture of casein is more refined, but still involves curdling milk in some way, often by adding acid.

The binding power of skim milk is low because it contains very little casein, so a lot of milk is required to make casein paint. Also, casein develops binding power only when an alkali is added to hydrolyze it, when it is turned to casein glue.

MAKING AMMONIUM CASEIN

1 *Place 1 part casein powder in a bowl and add 4 parts water. If larger amounts are needed a paint bucket can be used instead of a bowl.*

2 *Mix the casein powder and water together carefully so as to avoid creating any lumps or air bubbles.*

3 *When the solution is smooth, add approximately ½–1 part ammonium carbonate. The mixture will effervesce and become slightly sticky.*

4 *Allow the mixture to stand for about 30 minutes. Add a further 2–4 parts water, depending on the consistency required, and then add the pigment of your choice.*

This action is similar to making junket (a type of pudding) by adding rennet to milk. Casein paint is often called milk paint, but this term is not strictly correct; it should more accurately be called after the alkali to which it has been added – lime casein, ammonium casein, or borax casein.

The oldest known method of producing casein paint is with lime. The hydrolyzing agent is slaked lime putty. Lime casein has the advantage of being very stable and is particularly suited to painting lime plaster walls. (It is important to use alkaline-fast pigments. All earth pigments are suitable because they are inert.)

Lime casein makes a flat/mat paint with a rough texture. It is very permanent and does not need a primer. Colonial Americans and Shakers used to paint their furniture and walls with lime casein, as the materials were easily available – milk from the cow, and lime and pigments from the earth. When dry, lime casein is biodegradable, non-toxic, and solvent-free.

Ammonium casein is made from casein powder and ammonium carbonate. This produces a very transparent paint, so white pigment must be added to make it opaque. It can also be used as a woodstain. All casein paints use water as a thinner. Take care when making both ammonium and lime casein, as these alkalis are strong and can burn.

Casein paint is now available in small pots from art specialty stores. It is sometimes used in place of gouache paints as it is a hardy paint that can be applied very flatly. The strong, smooth surface that it provides has also led to it being used as an alternative to gesso under oil-gilding or Dutch metal effects.

Milk and lime paint

Ammonium carbonate

Materials and equipment
Various ingredients for making casein paints are shown here. Lime casein can be made simply from its basic ingredients or bought in powder form and reconstituted with water.

Separated milk

Water

Pigment

Casein binding medium

Casein powder (hydrochloric)

Mixing spoon

Brush

MIXING LIME CASEIN PAINT

1 *Add equal parts of water and lime casein powder. Keep stirring the mixture until the powder has been fully dispersed. The paint can then be thinned with water to the desired consistency.*

2 *Lime casein paint can be used on walls as well as furniture. The color changes slightly when dry (light paint becomes darker and vice versa), so it is best to make a test.*

The Furniture Painter's Techniques

♦ *Gesso* ♦ *Oil-gilding* ♦ *Bronze Powders* ♦
♦ *Lining* ♦ *Découpage* ♦ *Lacquer* ♦
♦ *Woodstains* ♦ *Varnishes* ♦
♦ *Liming* ♦

THE HIGH POINT in the art of painting furniture occurred in the 18th century, when a generation of highly-skilled craftsmen responded to the swift stylistic changes that interior decoration was undergoing at the time. It was an extravagant period when grand palaces and great houses were decorated with an opulence and splendor never seen before. The motifs and styles were broad ranging, but a constant theme was the workmanship and consummate skill of the builders, painters, cabinetmakers, gilders, and framers. Each craftsman was highly specialized and was responsible only for his particular area.

Roman architecture, which had already influenced the Renaissance and Baroque styles, was an inspirational force. It emerged again in Neoclassicism. Furniture was made from beautifully grained woods and was often enhanced by paintwork. Scenes were painted, sometimes in *grisaille*, in small areas such as panels or medallions. *Grisaille* is monochrome painting that simulates architectural features. Cherubs, trophies, classical subjects, and visions of Arcadia with Roman gods and goddesses, were among the most popular motifs. One of the most famous decorators was Angelica Kauffmann, the Swiss-born, 18th-century artist, who worked not only with the

A small cherub (left) taken from a popular book of découpage cut-outs was glued to an off-white background. After being varnished and then crackle varnished, dark oil colors were applied to the cracks to darken the overall effect.

architect Robert Adam but also with the furniture designer Thomas Hepplewhite.

Another strong influence on European furniture makers of the period was the importation of lacquerwork from the East. Europeans were fascinated by Oriental goods and a huge demand for Oriental furniture and artefacts developed. Craftsmen throughout Europe perfected techniques to simulate lacquerwork. One of these, called *vernis martin*, was developed in Paris by the Martin brothers in about 1730; this probably used shellac as a substitute for real lacquer. In the 1920s, Eileen Gray, working in Paris, used authentic orishi resin as well as other materials. She was the first lacquer artist to use modern designs. The demand for this chinoiserie fashion encouraged European artists at first to copy, and then later to find their own style of painting and decorating furniture. This influence is apparent in découpage work and decorated trays, which are produced today by craftsmen and home decorators alike.

The Neoclassical style encouraged furniture decorators and painters to use *faux-marbre* ("false marble") techniques. Later on, in the early 19th century, chests and cupboards were decorated with lines over plain or strié/dragged backgrounds. This lining technique is still used as a means of decoration on all types of painted furniture, and elevates an ordinary object to something special.

Distressing gold, silver, and copper leaf, applied over colored backgrounds, can achieve some remarkable effects (above). Try using warm colors under silver and cool golds, and cold blues under copper and the reddish golds.

There is a huge variety of gift wrap available (right) that can be used in découpage designs.

Gilding is a particularly specialized craft. It was carried out on furniture and frames, especially in the early 17th century. Metal leaf and bronze powder were used, sometimes over painted or lacquered gesso. A gilder's principle material is thin metal leaf and, as this was so expensive, the craft remained in the hands of highly-trained professionals. There is no rustic tradition in gilding as there is in painting. Nevertheless, oil-gilding techniques can be used to create a wide range of exciting finishes, and they are less demanding and exacting than those required for the highly-skilled technique of water-gilding.

Gesso was an important material for the furniture decorator, the framer, and the gilder. It provided a smooth surface which obscured inferior wood and other surfaces and was able to take metal leaf for gilding. The technique of mixing and applying gesso has not changed since the ancient Egyptians first used it. Using gesso and painting over cheaper wood, such as pine, is a traditional feature of furniture decoration. A notable example of this is Venetian painted furniture. Gesso is now used mainly by gilders and framers rather than furniture makers, perhaps because it is not able to withstand the knocks and bumps of modern life.

Woodgraining became very popular in the 19th century. Birdseye maple, burr walnut, and mahogany were popular woods for this technique.

Particular styles of painted furniture developed all over Europe, and especially where there was an abundance of wood. The Swedes, for example, who have a strong tradition of painted furniture, developed a distinctive style during the reign of King Gustav in the 18th century. Most decorative furniture was painted in the classical, traditional style, but some, such as the English artists of the Omega workshop, open from 1913 to 1919, used paint and color in a freer, more spontaneous and expressive way.

There is also a rich tradition of painted furniture in peasant culture, which originated in Europe but soon found its own motifs and characteristic style in

A metal tray has been decorated with modern découpage (left). The tray was first painted black and then cut-outs from magazines were added to create a random collage effect. The whole tray was varnished with many coats both to provide protection and to achieve an even surface.

both North and South America. This naive and sometimes crude style is found all over the world, notably in South America and India. This peasant farmhouse painting is often in imitation of the grander pieces seen in large houses. Woodgraining and marbling, for instance, were often imitated and carried out in a crude manner. The style in North America has its roots especially in German painted furniture and English bronze powder lacquerwork. These pieces, whether they are Pennsylvanian Dutch or French Provincial, have all developed their own strong, indigenous, and individual styles. Very often, simple paints and stenciled motifs based on natural forms were used.

More recently, decorative artists have used these farmhouse styles and incorporated them in modern pieces. Apart from the professional craftsmen, there are the untrained and sometimes amateur decorators who work outside the mainstream classical style. The attraction of furniture decoration is the wide range of techniques and skills it encompasses. Découpage, for instance, allows you to work with pictures and images, without being able to draw, while gilding involves using exciting materials to produce spectacular results.

This lamp base (above) has been painted with a milk paint which includes lime. The lime gives it a soft, slightly powdery look and provides a very robust finish.

Metal leaf for gilding comes in small books such as these (left), each leaf protected by tissue paper. In the 1920s, particularly in France, quite large pieces of furniture, such as cabinets and chests, were covered in silver leaf, broken only by the lines of the piece or some lacquered design.

Gesso

GESSO HAS A long history in furniture decoration. The recipe that is used today is similar to that used by the ancient Egyptians. It creates an extremely smooth and porous surface. Being porous, it allows paint, lacquer, or size to be absorbed without soaking in completely. It is used under water-gilding, so that the gold leaf may be burnished without tearing, and under oil-gilding, particularly on carved pine items where the wood is a little rough. In both types of gilding, the gesso is often first colored with a red or yellow clay, known as bole, so as to give a good background color. It is also used in lacquer work, where a smooth surface is essential.

As a decorating surface it is most commonly found on frames, decorative items, and furniture, particularly those of Venetian furniture painters. Objects that have been gessoed and then decorated can sometimes be identified when scratches and knocks reveal a layer of white underneath a painted or gilded surface.

When it is thoroughly dry, gesso can also be carved. In the 18th and 19th centuries, gesso was used to imitate the intricate carving found on Oriental lacquer pieces.

Gesso is a white liquid made from a fine white chalk, known as whiting, mixed with size or glue made from rabbitskin. Rabbitskin glue is available in granules and sheets from most art shops; artists also use the glue to size their canvases. To use gesso, you simply brush it onto a surface and build it up in layers. Each layer should be lightly sanded before the next layer is applied.

Gesso is quite easy to prepare. The rabbitskin granules are soaked in water and melted down to make the glue or size. On cooling, it solidifies into a gel. This can be liquefied again by reheating over a double boiler. Once made up, it has a limited life. Excess should be stored in the refrigerator, but it tends to thicken. Diluting with water is unsatisfactory as it makes a weaker solution; it is better to make fresh mixtures as you need them.

Gesso can be made up in varying proportions of whiting to glue size. Generally, though, whiting is added to the glue size until it has absorbed all the liquid. When the mixture is stirred, it becomes liquid. The greater your skill, the more whiting you may add. A thicker mixture dries fairly quickly but is more prone to air bubbles which disturb the smooth surface.

The versatility of gesso
These examples demonstrate the flexibility of gesso. The example (right) has been combed before the gesso dried. The following technique was used on the small chest of drawers (opposite). Cotton cloth was painted with layers of gesso which were allowed to dry between applications. After five thin coats, the cloth was pulled across the corner of a table to crack the gesso. A mixture of pigment, polyvinyl acrylic/PVA, and water was rubbed into the cracks. The cloth was then cut and glued to the chest of drawers.

An alternative to classic or traditional gesso is an acrylic polymer gesso which can be purchased at any art supply store. It can be thinned with water and should be applied to the surface in layers, sanding between applications. You can also make an imitation version using equal parts of water and polyvinyl acrylic/PVA. Then add the whiting until there is no more liquid to be absorbed, before stirring it in. These alternatives do, however, have slightly different properties. Unlike traditional gesso, they are too hard to cut and mold, and, being nonabsorbent, a far shinier surface is created when they are painted over.

Pigment can also be added to classic and imitation gesso to color the final coats. A surface which is to be gessoed should first be coated with a thin solution of hot rabbitskin glue size. Glue size can also be used in making paint, when it acts as the binder for pigment (*see pages 132–135*).

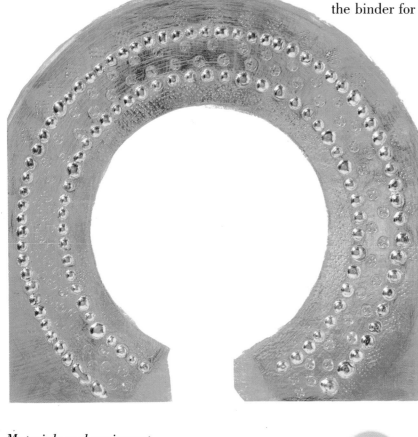

Using gesso in decoration
Gold leaf which has been water-gilded onto gesso presents a more adaptable surface. Here (left) the gold leaf has been decorated using punches. This is possible only with water-gilding. Gesso can also be built up into decorative shapes (above).

Materials and equipment
These are the ingredients used to make gesso. It is basically a mix of whiting and rabbitskin glue size and follows a simple recipe which has remained the same for centuries.

Gesso

Gesso brush

Water

Rabbitskin granules (melted)

Rabbitskin granules (raw)

Saucepan

Whiting

Pantyhose for straining the gesso mixture

MIXING AND USING GESSO

1 Soak the rabbitskin granules overnight in cold water. Use 1 part granules to 10 parts water.

2 Add a further 10 parts water in the morning. Place the bowl in a pan of hot water or double boiler and stir until the granules have dissolved.

3 Add whiting to the melted granules, continuing until the whiting has absorbed all the liquid. Stir until it reverts to a liquid form.

4 Strain the liquid through nylon mesh (such as old pantyhose) stretched over a clean bowl and let it drip through.

5 Sand the surface to be gessoed and size it with melted glue size. Allow to dry for several hours. Paint the first thin layer of gesso onto the surface, always working the brush in the same direction.

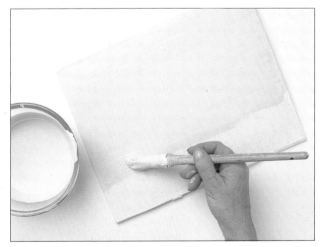

6 When the first layer has dried, apply a thin, second layer, working the brush in the opposite direction. Apply a minimum of five coats, sanding lightly between applications.

Oil-gilding

GILDING IS THE application of gold, silver, or other metal leaf to surfaces. It is a craft which has changed little over the centuries. There are two methods: oil-gilding and water-gilding. Water-gilding is a highly skilled art and not within this book's scope. The main difference in appearance is that water-gilding can be polished with a burnisher and so appears much brighter.

The leaf used for oil-gilding is gold, silver, aluminum, copper, palladium, and a gold-colored metal leaf called Dutch metal or Dutch gold. They are available in the forms of loose leaf and transfer leaf. Transfer leaf consists of sheets of beaten metal pressed onto waxed tissue paper.

Oil-gilding requires a smooth, hard surface. This may be gesso, but a smooth ground which has been sprayed or painted and sanded between coats may also be used. Faults in the surface will show all imperfections and tear the wafer-thin metal, so surfaces should be well prepared, sanded smooth, and painted with an oil basecoat. You can use spray paint which covers the surface quickly and evenly and reaches awkward corners without any risk of dripping. The leaf is secured to the surface by means of a mordant made from linseed oil, called gold size. Gold size that dries at different rates, varying from less than an hour to 24 hours, is available. The surface is painted with gold size and when it is dry, or very nearly dry, the leaf is laid and very gently rubbed down until the backing paper can be peeled off. Knowing when the gold size is ready for the leaf to be applied is a matter of judgment. You can experiment with a small hidden area before you begin.

In the 18th century, gold was laid directly onto the wooden frame without gesso, and 19th-century, Pre-Raphaelite artists favored frames where the oil-gilding was laid straight onto oak so the grain showed through. The water-gilding method was always used on frames and interior moldings in France and Italy, but in Britain, oil-gilding was used, perhaps because it could withstand the damp atmosphere.

A basic technique for laying down a sheet of metal leaf is described here. This is followed by three distressing techniques. Distressing gilding has always been part of the gilder's craft. Here, some of the basic techniques have been exaggerated. Metal leaf is adhered to a base color and then painted over with a sponge, scratched back with sandpaper, or tarnished with a chemical solution. These techniques can be used on a wide variety of metals to produce a myriad of effects.

Eggshell, Japan paints/japlac, or gloss oil paint may be used for the basecoat. Its color is important as these metals have an aura of richness which is heightened by strong and sumptuous colors.

Techniques using chemical solutions are never entirely predictable and often oxidation means that

Richness and variety
These eggs and spheres were oil-gilded and then distressed by artist Tennille Dix-Amzallag. Their differences stem from varying the base color, type of metal leaf, and the strength of chemical solutions.

the effect continues to change even months after the surface has been sealed. Copper and metal leaf can be distressed by adding household bleach; this reacts within about four hours. Salt water can be added to copper leaf to make a verdigris finish.

Most of the materials used today are as ancient as the craft of gilding itself. In oil-gilding, thin sheets of gold or other metal leaf are stuck to a surface with gold size. Originally, gold size was oxidized using raw linseed oil. The recipe varied according to the drying time required. The size is left to dry until it becomes tacky and is ready to receive the metal leaf. Different rates of drying enable a craftsman to work over large areas. Once the gold size is too dry, the leaf will not stick.

Nowadays, Japan gold size is a quick-drying gold size made of a clear, synthetic varnish. It dries completely and loses its tack in about 30 minutes. Adding oil size to it slows the drying time. Japan gold size is convenient for doing small pieces of gilding, and fine work can be undertaken with greater accuracy because it is not so thick as ordinary size. In both cases, size should be applied to a nonabsorbent surface, such as shellac or eggshell. Shellac remains nonabsorbent even after it has been rubbed down.

Luster powders
Powders containing mica to give luster are available in many colors (right and below). They are also available in liquid form.

Luster powders

Bronze powders
These fine metallic powders (right) are called bronze powders even though they are made from copper, silver, aluminum, or alloys. They need to be protected from oxidation with lacquer or varnish.

Bronze powders

Gesso brushes
Although any brush can be used to apply gesso, traditionally, gesso brushes (right) do not have metal ferrules which would rust.

Gesso brushes

Rabbitskin glue
Rabbitskin granules (left) or sheet (below) are used in conjunction with whiting to make gesso. This provides an extremely smooth surface which is used for both oil- and water-gilding.

Rabbitskin granules

Whiting
Natural calcium carbonate ground to a fine powder (above) is used to make gesso. It is available in various grades.

Rabbitskin sheet

Liquid gold
Also known as gold varnish, this (below) is bronze powder suspended in a medium. It must be shaken frequently to prevent the powder from sinking to the bottom.

Liquid gold

Gold transfer leaf

Silver transfer leaf

Aluminum transfer leaf

Metal leaf
This is available as loose or transfer leaf (above and left). Aluminum leaf, known as white metal, is not so shiny as other metals. Like real gold, aluminum does not tarnish, but Dutch metal, silver, and copper leaf do, and they need to be varnished or lacquered to prevent the process.

Gilder's tamper

Dutch gold transfer leaf

Copper loose leaf

Nonluster metallic powders

Gilt creams
These (below) are fine soft waxes colored with bronze powders. When gilt creams have dried, they can be buffed to a shine. They are available in many colors and can be used for stenciling.

Gilt creams

Gold size
This (below right) is used in oil-gilding to adhere the metal leaf onto the surface. Gold size is available in many different drying times, from 30 minutes to 24 hours.

Nonluster metallic powders
These powders (above) are made from colored aluminum.

Gold size

Materials and equipment
These are the materials needed for the techniques of oil-gilding and distressing the applied metallic leaf which are described on the following pages.

Book of transfer metal leaf

Protective gloves

Paper towels

Potassium sulfide

Gilder's tamper

Base paint and brush

Mineral spirits/ white spirit

Oil-free, fine grade steelwool

Gold size

Oil paint

Shellac

Tack cloth

Sponges

APPLYING SILVER LEAF

1 Cover the surface with a base color. Here, black lacquer paint is used, but it may be any color. Spray paints also work well.

2 Wipe the surface with a tack cloth to remove any dust. Dust must be removed as it will tear the leaf and show through.

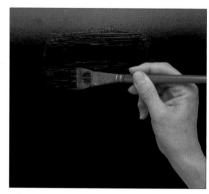

3 Apply the gold size with a stiff bristle, short-haired brush. It should be well brushed out so that a thin, even layer covers the surface.

4 Allow the gold size to dry, testing it with your knuckle on a hidden area. The size should have the same dry tack as the adhesive side of tape.

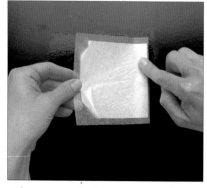

5 Lay a page of silver leaf gently over the size. Rub down gently starting in one corner and working backward and forward.

6 Press the leaf gently with a gilder's tamper or absorbent cotton/cotton wool to ensure adherence and to remove any air bubbles.

GILDING A CANDLESTICK

1 *This shows how to apply leaf to an irregular surface. Complete the first four steps on the preceding page. Cut a strip of metal leaf from the sheet; apply it to the base of the candlestick.*

2 *Gently push the silver leaf well into the crevices with your fingertips or a gilder's tamper. If there are gaps or tears, fill them in with any remaining scraps of silver leaf.*

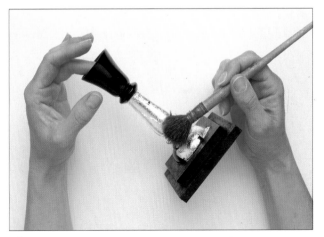

3 *Dab the silver leaf all over with a gilder's tamper or absorbent cotton/cotton wool, ensuring that it has adhered firmly and that there are no air bubbles. Repeat the process until the whole object is covered.*

Gilded and distressed lamp
Potassium sulfide has been applied over copper leaf on a wooden candlestick and a metal lampshade (left), to great effect.

Finishing effects

These samples show the richness and the variety which can be achieved with a few techniques using a combination of different methods, metals, and colors.

Distressed silver leaf

Silver leaf (below) on a gloss black base was distressed with a strong solution of potassium sulfide (1:6). These effects continue to change under oxidation.

Distressed Dutch leaf

This leaf (above) was distressed first with cupric nitrate then rubbed down lightly with steelwool. It was wiped clean to halt the process.

DUTCH METAL

1 Paint a thin layer of shellac over Dutch metal. This acts as a barrier between the leaf and the paint. Paint the shellac in one application, using a soft brush.

2 Mix some artist's oil paint with a little mineral spirits/white spirit to dilute it. Dip a sponge into the paint and dab it over the leaf.

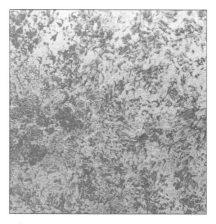

3 The finished effect – more paint can be applied to obscure more of the Dutch metal. Alternatively, another color can be used.

Distressed Dutch metal
This (left) was distressed by "puddling" on cupric nitrate, which eats away at the leaf. It was then rinsed gently in water to stop oxidation.

Distressed Dutch leaf
Dutch leaf (below) was applied over a gloss Vermilion paint and distressed lightly by using a sponge dipped in a weak solution of potassium sulfide.

Distressed copper leaf
A copper base (right) has been distressed with a weak solution of cupric nitrate, which has been "puddled" in parts to provide a more intense effect.

Distressed copper leaf
The metal leaf (left) was distressed with a full strength solution of sodium sulfide which was applied with a sponge.

Distressed Dutch metal
Cupric nitrate was sponged on and left overnight to eat away at the metal leaf (below).

Spheres and eggs
These (above and right) are some of the objects on which these techniques can be applied.

DISTRESSING DUTCH METAL

1 Layer the Dutch metal on a black ground. Rub it down with fine steelwool (0000-grade) dipped in mineral spirits/white spirit.

2 Rub the leaf gently with a paper towel dipped in mineral spirits/white spirit.

3 Apply three coats of polyurethane varnish, allowing them to dry in between applications, to protect the final piece.

USING POTASSIUM SULFIDE

1 *Wearing protective gloves, dissolve a pea-size lump of potassium sulfide in 4 teaspoons of water. Weaker or stronger solutions will have a different effect. Handle with extreme caution; it is caustic and corrosive.*

2 *Using a sponge, apply the solution to the leaf: the stronger the solution, the harsher the effect.*

3 *Protect the final piece with polyurethane varnish, applying three coats, allowing them to dry between applications.*

Distressed copper leaf
Copper leaf (left) was simply sponged with barium until the desired effect was achieved.

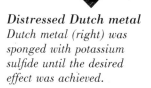

Distressed Dutch metal
Dutch metal (right) was sponged with potassium sulfide until the desired effect was achieved.

Bronze Powders

THE ANCIENT Chinese first used bronze powders in their lacquer work, employing a method similar to that shown here. Bronze powders were also sprinkled lightly between the layered lacquered surfaces to add luster, a technique also used in 18th-century France by the Martin brothers, French craftsmen patronized by Louis XV.

Bronze powders are intended to resemble the many different colors of gold, which is too expensive for most people to use. Despite their name, they are made from the very fine, dust-like powder of various metals, such as copper and zinc. Unlike true gold, the metals tarnish, so bronze powders need fixing with a suitable substance, such as shellac. The powders may also be mixed with gum arabic and painted on, but they still need to be sealed to prevent oxidation.

Objects in everyday use, such as trays, should be coated with shellac and then covered with several layers of polyurethane to protect them from heat. Acrylic varnish may also be used.

Motif with bronze powders
Bronze powders are available in a wide range of colors. Three or four colors are the maximum that can pleasingly be used on one piece (above).

Materials and equipment
All these materials are available from good artist's suppliers. The possible exceptions may be the powders and gold size. These may be obtained from suppliers of gilder's materials.

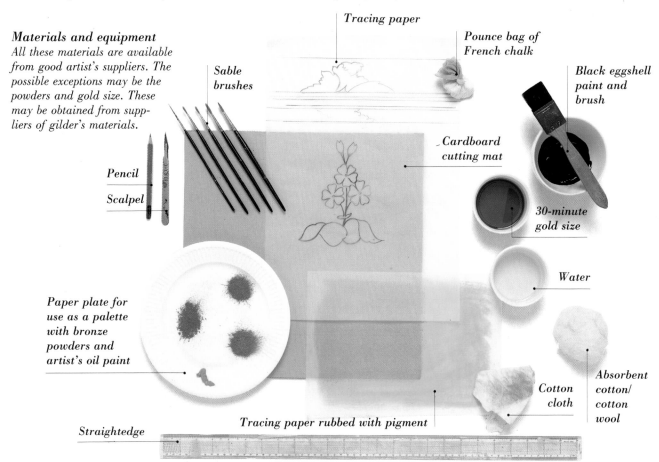

Tracing paper

Pounce bag of French chalk

Black eggshell paint and brush

Sable brushes

Cardboard cutting mat

Pencil

Scalpel

30-minute gold size

Water

Paper plate for use as a palette with bronze powders and artist's oil paint

Absorbent cotton/ cotton wool

Cotton cloth

Straightedge

Tracing paper rubbed with pigment

APPLYING BRONZE POWDERS

1 *Either design your own pattern or trace or draw a clear, simple pattern from a copyright-free book onto tracing paper with a sharp soft pencil.*

2 *Make "carbon paper" by rubbing light colored pigment over another sheet of tracing paper with a cotton cloth.*

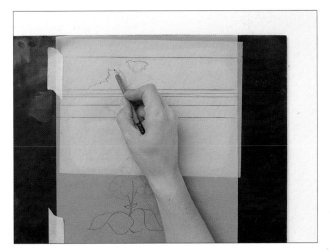

3 *Make a pounce bag from nylon pantyhose and fill it with French chalk. Rub it all over the surface to be decorated to degrease it.*

4 *Place the tracing over the "carbon paper," pigment side down, and secure with masking tape. Trace over the drawing, moving the paper along for repeats.*

5 *Check that sufficient pressure has been used to make sure the drawing is transferred.*

6 *Pour a little size onto a paper plate. Work the excess off a sable brush and apply a very thin layer over areas of the bronzing surface that do not touch.*

(Continued on page 106)

7 *Using another sable brush, apply the bronze powder over one edge. Feather it out as shown.*

8 *Continue to work across the surface. Apply the size to alternate areas. This ensures that excess bronze powder does not adhere to the wrong areas when feathered out.*

9 *Dip a piece of absorbent cotton/cotton wool in water and wipe off excess powder. If needed, add a drop of dish-washing liquid to the water.*

10 *Pounce the surface with French chalk. Sized areas are still sticky and need protection from bronze powder applied at the next stage.*

11 *Fill in the unsized and unpowdered areas as before. Wiping with water deletes the lines, so they may have to be redrawn.*

12 *Paint the lines with oil size and apply the bronze powder. Wipe with water and pounce with French chalk again.*

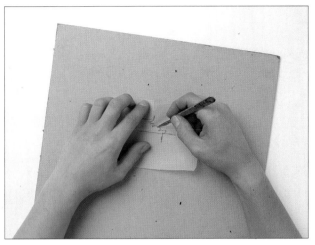

13 *When repeating a pattern, create a tracing paper stencil by tracing the pattern to be repeated on a separate sheet of tracing paper.*

14 *Cut out the edge with a scalpel on a sheet of cardboard or a cutting mat to create a stencil.*

15 *Paint a wide strip of gold size along the stencil. Lay the stencil down, brush bronze powder over the edge and feather it out. Repeat until complete.*

16 *Mix artist's oil paint with a little gold size and, using a straightedge and your fingers to guide you, paint the lines.*

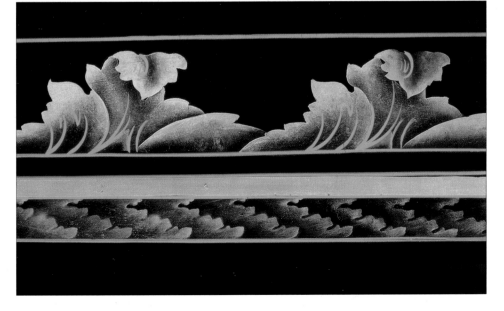

The finished border
This border design (left) could, for example, be used around the edge of a tray, with another motif appearing in the center. The feathering technique uses only small amounts of bronze powder and so a little goes a long way. The repeat use of the tracing paper stencil is quick to execute, and the light orange lines add a finishing touch.

Lining

LINING IS THE art of making lines on walls and on furniture. It is a very simple way of making an ordinary piece of furniture look more elegant. The skill lies in mixing the paint to the correct consistency and in drawing straight lines of an appropriate width and color.

The brushes used vary according to the craftsman's preference. Traditional lining brushes are made with longer hairs to hold the maximum amount of paint.

Lines are drawn by hand and eye rather than measured with a ruler. A craftsman uses the edge of the furniture as a visual guide. He also uses the fingers that are not gripping the brush to guide his hand along the edge. Only when the line is too far in from the edge will he resort to a straightedge to act as a guide.

When painting lines wider than $\frac{1}{4}$ inch/6 mm, it is usual to paint two lines and then fill them in with another brush. To get wide or thin lines, the pressure applied to the brush is varied.

Artist's oil paint is used as it does not dry so quickly. Mistakes can be wiped off while still wet. Mix up sufficient paint in advance. It should be thin enough to flow well, but opaque enough to cover the surface. Adding a little white helps to make it opaque, especially with some colors. If it is too thick, it will not flow properly, but if it is too

MAKING LINES ON A TABLE

1 Guide lines are drawn freehand with a colored pencil. Use a light color on dark grounds and vice versa so that the lines are clearly visible.

2 Mix paint and varnish and load the brush well. Use your third finger to guide the brush and your little or ring finger to guide your hand.

3 A thin dark line is added to indicate a shadow. If the brush runs out of paint, restart the line before the break and rejoin the flow of the line.

4 An ocher line adds a finishing touch. It is advisable for beginners to wait until each line is dry before starting the next so that mistakes can be wiped off.

*Piece of wood to act
as a straightedge*

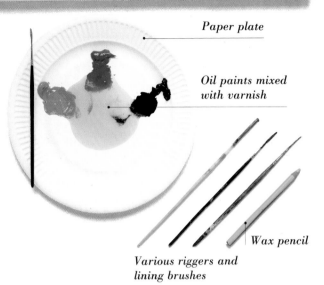

Paper plate

*Oil paints mixed
with varnish*

thin, it will run. Mixing paint with varnish helps to create the right consistency. The varnish increases the flow and the viscosity of the paint without diluting it. Some craftsmen add gold size instead of varnish to the paint to speed up the drying time.

If you have to stop and restart a line, work back into it gradually. Retrace your loaded brush along the direction of the old line before you allow it to make a mark, and then gradually increase the pressure so that the line regains the correct width.

*Materials and equipment
A wax pencil shows up better on
a dark surface. The straightedge
used should be heavy enough
to discourage movement and
prevent slipping.*

Wax pencil

*Various riggers and
lining brushes*

5 *This shows the different position for holding the hand to draw a line further in from the edge of the table.*

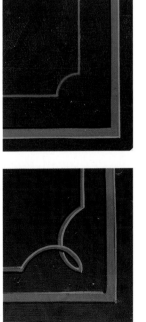

6 *A straight piece of wood is used to guide the hand since the line is too far away from the edge of the table to be painted comfortably.*

Corner designs
These examples by François Lavenir (below) show a variety of corner designs. Each craftsman develops his or her own methods to facilitate the drawing of lines. Some of these designs are painted by using the hand as a compass. The little finger is placed in the center of an imaginary circle and used as a pivot. Good lining is a matter of practice and confidence. Lines drawn too slowly may wobble. Lines drawn quickly and without care can look sloppy. Keep a controlled speed and maintain even pressure, otherwise the line will become alternately thick and thin. Keep a cotton cloth at hand so mistakes can be wiped off.

Découpage

ÉCOUPAGE IS A method of decorating trays, boxes, walls, furniture, screens, lampshades, and many more objects with paper cut-outs stuck onto the surface and then given a protective layer of varnish or lacquer. It is a deceptively simple but effective technique, which needs precision, care, and attention to detail, color, and design.

Découpage has a long tradition as a decorating technique and can be used on any hard, painted surface, such as wood and metal. It has close links with the art of lacquer (*see pages 114–115*). Decorated furniture became very fashionable in the 17th and 18th centuries, popularized by lacquerware coming from the Far East.

To keep up with the high demand, small paper cut-outs were printed as a substitute for the very time-consuming method of hand painting. All the cut-outs were colored by hand and were varnished many times, usually with a resin spirit varnish called sandarac. The art of good découpage lies in careful cutting of the paper and applying very many layers of varnish.

Sources for découpage can be found in facsimile editions, which are sometimes copyright-free and can, therefore, be photocopied. As early as 1762,

The Print Room, Rokeby Park, Yorkshire, England
From the 1750s until the mid-19th century, pasting walls with engravings and cut-out printed paper swags and borders was a very popular way of decorating interiors. Sometimes unusual colors were used for the background – strong pink, straw, or gray, for example. The pink color shown here was quite uncommon.

books like *The Ladies Amusement* or the *Art of Japanning*, with 1,500 illustrations for cutting out, were being published. Today, greeting cards, old books, theater programs, and gift wrap are also good sources. Black and white and colored photocopies are also possibilities. There are some books specifically for découpage still being published and these are often good sources for classical motifs, such as architectural details, cherubs, and bows. Magazines can be used, but the pages should be tested as they are sometimes so thin that the glue and/or the varnish makes the underside of the page show through.

Traditionally, the background was a plain color, often green or black, sometimes Yellow Ocher, and, occasionally, red. It can be painted many colors or with different effects, including marbling, woodgraining, and other glazed effects.

Découpage was popular in 18th-century France, where it was called *scriban* (the art of the desk). Venetian craftsmen called it *arte povra*, but it has also been known as *lacca povra*, *lacca contrafatta* when the surface was lacquered, and by the more descriptive name of découpage.

By the 19th century, it had become a hobby for Victorian ladies, and at that time pieces of chintz fabric were also being used for decorating furniture. Because of its background of Oriental decoration, chinoiserie has always been a popular subject. The finish may be crackle varnished (*see pages 146–147*) to make the work look like an old painting. The basecoat may be any paint – water or oil – but oil is easier to use.

Possibly as a result of using découpage on small objects, people began to use prints to decorate rooms to create what are now known as print rooms. Sometimes a theme was chosen and was used throughout the room.

When cutting out your chosen image, use sharp, fine scissors and keep moving the paper so that you are always cutting away from you and your hand is never in an awkward position. You can also use a

Venetian chair
This chair (above) is a fine example of arte povra *and is decorated in the unusual colors of red and yellow. This is a result of the direct influence of Oriental lacquer work. The detail (right) demonstrates how the many layers of lacquer or varnish disguise the découpage.*

scalpel knife with a fine blade, or a craft knife, but you need a proper cutting surface. Again, the paper should be turned all the time so that you are always drawing the blade toward you and not holding it at an awkward angle.

Make sure that each stage has been satisfactorily completed before starting the next. Check that all the edges are securely stuck down before varnishing or sealing. This is most important, as the loose edge will deteriorate if it is not rectified at this stage. For an oil-based background, the best glue to use is a mucilage glue, as the excess can be easily wiped off. Allow it to dry overnight before applying the varnish or lacquer.

Here we show Tennille Dix-Amzallag's method of decorating a metal tray. The tray was given a basecoat with spray paint, used for its quick-drying properties, ease and speed of application, and tough surface. A quick-drying lacquer paint or gloss paint would also do. Make sure the brush and the surface are dust free if you want to achieve a silky, smooth effect. In the final stages, the tray was given 15 coats of varnish to ensure that it would be heat-resistant. The varnish, which can be polyurethane or acrylic, also hides the edges of the paper and the fact that the paper flowers and butterfly are glued on. Every third coat should be sanded down with a fine grade paper and wiped with a tack cloth before the next coat is applied.

Materials and equipment
All these materials, with the exception of the tack cloth, are easy to obtain. The books are published for the purposes of découpage, and interesting gift wrap can be bought at stationery stores and museum shops.

Metal tray

Mucilage glue

Small scissors

Gift wrap

Black spray paint

Clear varnish and flat brush

Natural sponge

Tack cloth

Woven paper cloth

Cellulose sponge

Source books

DECORATING A TRAY

1 Plan your design, then roughly cut out the image with a small pair of fine scissors. Trim off excess paper around the image.

2 Carefully cut out the image, moving the paper so that you are cutting directly away from yourself. Have ready water, glue, and a damp, well squeezed-out cellulose sponge.

3 Spread the glue onto the tray with your finger. The glue can be thinned with water to give an oily, buttery, even consistency. Mucilage glue or gum adhesive is best.

4 Position the paper carefully and stick it down, using the sponge with a dabbing motion. Do not use a sweeping action which might dislodge the picture or even tear it.

5 Remove all traces of glue with a wet sponge and dab with a dry cloth to remove any moisture. Do not rub or disturb the paper. Air bubbles disappear as the paper dries.

6 Allow to dry overnight. Check that edges are firmly stuck down. Wipe with a tack cloth, and varnish. This brush should be kept only for varnishing. The last coat may be waxed or left as it is.

Lacquer

GENUINE ORIENTAL lacquer is made from a resin harvested from the orishi tree, which is native to both Japan and China. It is produced by the Cocca lacca insect, which penetrates the bark of the tree and deposits the lac, the raw material for lacquer.

Applying lacquer was a painstaking process requiring great skill and patience. The resin was thickened by evaporation, then strained, and colored with pigments. As many as 30 to 40 thin coats were applied to an object. Each layer had to be perfectly even and dry before being rubbed down prior to applying the next coat. The resulting dense, hard, smooth surface was ideal for gilding, carving, and inlay. The beauty of the finished lacquer piece is derived from the way in which light is refracted through the layers of lac.

The term lacquer is sometimes used to apply to any surface coated with a shiny, varnished paint; but to do this is to disregard the unique look that true lacquer offers. Many attempts have been made to imitate this look with other, less time-consuming techniques. None, however, have succeeded.

The art of lacquering originated in the East and lacquered pieces found their way to the West as early as the 17th century. It became a more familiar skill among Western artists during the Art Deco period (late 1920s and 1930s), when many Japanese came to the West to work. The designs on lacquered pieces tend, even today, to reflect the oriental origins of the art, but there have been some notable exceptions. During the Art Deco period many lacquered pieces had striking, geometric designs. A key exponent of the art at this time was the Irishwoman Eileen Gray, who is particularly known for her very finely finished lacquer screens and other pieces of furniture, which possess an extraordinary depth of color. She worked first with traditional orishi resin, but then formulated her own techniques, using shellac as a substitute.

Today all Western lacquer technique uses shellac instead of orishi resin. This is not least because orishi resin is poisonous and prolonged exposure to it causes an allergic reaction. Shellac is taken from *Rhus verniciflua*, a tree which grows in the Far East, and looks similar to true lacquer. Shellac, also known as lac (hence the word lacquer), can be bought in the form of brittle crystal-like flakes or as a liquid. There are many grades; the less refined is used for lacquerwork. The flakes are dissolved in alcohol to make a usable varnish.

There are many ready-mixed shellacs available, such as button-lac and garnet-lac. These are different types of shellac and tend to be very brittle. The hardest shellacs are de-waxed. Lacquer artists now use extra fine, clear polish or shellac, applied very thinly with a wad (a piece of absorbent cotton/cotton wool with cotton wrapped around it) and rubbed down between layers. There are many different recipes for making lacquer, but it should be stressed that perfection lies more in the care and attention taken in applying the lacquer than in the type of lacquer employed.

A simple method is to paint the surface with an oil-based undercoat and, when dry, rub it down with fine grade sandpaper to a very smooth finish. Finely ground pigments are then mixed with good quality, highly transparent shellac. The first coats contain a lot of pigment so that they are more opaque; the following coats contain a higher proportion of varnish or shellac. There should be many thin applications of lacquer, each evenly rubbed down when dry. Remember that only the layers of clear shellac should be rubbed down. If you rub down a layer of pigment and shellac the pigment will be lost.

Traditionally, most lacquer work was carried out on a black background, but Vermilion, dark green, and a white were also used.

Ducks
This small lacquer panel (above) was copied from an original piece with oil-gilding and hand-painted watercolor decoration on the ducks and flowers.

Materials and equipment

Shellac in liquid form is readily available, but can be made by mixing shellac flakes with pure alcohol or clear denatured alcohol/methylated spirits as shown below in Step 1. After application, shellac dries extremely quickly but takes far longer to harden throughout. For ideal results it should be left for 12 hours before being sanded. The color of the pigment can be changed slightly for subsequent layers (for example Venetian Red and Burnt Umber may be used alternately). This means you are looking through layers of different transparent colors to an opaque ground.

Shellac in liquid form

Two flat-ended brushes

Red Oxide pigment

APPLYING SHELLAC

1 Mix shellac with pure alcohol or clear denatured alcohol/methylated spirits, or use ready-mixed shellac.

2 Work shellac into the pigment to color it. At this stage the shellac and pigment can be ground smooth using a pestle and mortar.

3 Cover a gessoed object with a thin layer of the pigment mixed with shellac. Work the brush in one direction only. Allow to dry, but do not rub down.

4 Cover with a layer of clear shellac. When it is dry, rub smooth. Repeat applications of clear or pigmented shellac until the desired result is achieved.

Woodstains

WOODSTAINS ARE transparent liquids which allow the grain of the wood to show through the color. Reasons for staining may be to imitate a more exotic wood, match another wood, improve or emphasize the grain, or simply for color and decoration.

A large number of stains have been invented over the years. Many classic recipes use plant dyes such as logwood. Some of them sound as though they have come from the alchemist's workshop with ingredients such as dragon's blood, gallnuts/nut galls, and alkenet root (*see pages 44–45*). In the 17th century, pearwood frames were stained black to imitate ebony. Ebonizing was also popular with the Victorians, who used sycamore, plane, and chestnut wood, particularly for furniture. They also imitated other woods, such as mahogany, rose-wood, walnut, and cherry. Pine wood that was as plain and unfigured as possible was used. Mahogany-stained pine would have had the correct color but the wrong grain, and this led to craftsmen adding grain and combing. Many people considered this to be a debased form of woodgraining and painting.

Stains are usually applied only to new wood because staining stripped wood may result in unevenness. The stain can be applied directly onto untreated wood, but the result may be patchy and mottled. If a very even effect is needed, the wood should be sized. Use a mixture of turpentine and gold size for spirit-based stains, and a thin wash of rabbitskin glue size or thinned-down acrylic varnish for water-based stains. Apply rapidly with a large brush to ensure the surface is completely covered. Before you start the work, the wood should be well sanded. It is also advisable to test the strength of the woodstain on a hidden area first. Woodstains soak into the fabric of the wood, so if the stain is too concentrated in color, it cannot be easily removed by sanding down or stripping as with paints and varnishes.

Many of the old stains were applied sparingly and well rubbed in. The desired depth of color was obtained by using several washes rather than one, to bring out the natural grain.

Stained wood can be left plain, or finished by varnishing or waxing.

Shaker box
Shakers made a woodstain by boiling water and pigments together – in effect, a dye. The stain was brushed onto bare wood and later waxed. A copy of a Shaker box (above) has been treated in this way.

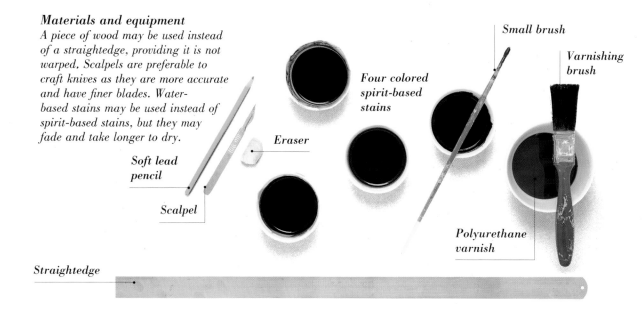

Materials and equipment
A piece of wood may be used instead of a straightedge, providing it is not warped. Scalpels are preferable to craft knives as they are more accurate and have finer blades. Water-based stains may be used instead of spirit-based stains, but they may fade and take longer to dry.

Soft lead pencil

Scalpel

Eraser

Four colored spirit-based stains

Small brush

Varnishing brush

Polyurethane varnish

Straightedge

Water stains

There were many woodstains which were made with recipes using natural materials. The following recipe is for a black stain.

Add 1 lb/450 g logwood and 2 or 3 handfuls of walnut shells to 14 cups/3.4 liters water. Boil vigorously until reduced by about half. Strain and add 2½ cups/600 ml white vinegar, boil again and apply the stain while still hot. Meanwhile, dissolve 1 oz/28 g copperas in 4 cups/1.2 liters water and apply while it is still hot over the previous stain. A combination of Burnt Sienna and beer made a mahogany stain, while a handful of rusty nails left in vinegar (acetic acid) made a stain to turn oak black. In medieval England, using ingredients like rusty nails was not uncommon. In the 18th century, box wood recorders were decorated with a stain using equal amounts of saltpeter and iron sulfide together with rusty nails, which were presumably left in the mixture to give it its color. As the recorders were handled frequently they could not be decorated with paint, so were stained in this way to make them look like tortoiseshell. To create this effect, the liquid would have been dropped on the recorder in spots.

WOODSTAIN DESIGN

1 Draw an accurate design in pencil. Make a slight cut over the lines with a sharp scalpel. This prevents the stains from seeping into other areas.

2 Fill in the design with woodstain using a fine brush. Spirit-based stains, which dry quickly, were used here.

3 Fill in the bigger areas with a larger brush. A dark border finishes the design.

4 Several coats of polyurethane varnish increase the depth of the colors and give protection.

Varnishes

VARNISH GIVES A protective coat to surfaces and also brings life to colors by giving them more depth and brilliance. A varnish can alter the appearance of a finish quite dramatically, and should enhance the finish as well as protect it. Varnishes may be either flat/mat or glossy; sometimes a colored stain is incorporated into the varnish to give it a decorative finish.

Contemporary varnishes are based on synthetic resins and are water-based; they are tough, dry quickly, and are non-yellowing. Acrylic varnishes have largely superseded the oil-based polyurethane varnishes for these reasons. Besides water- and oil-based varnishes, there are spirit-based varnishes, of which the best known is shellac.

Classic varnishes have a number of individual characteristics which set them apart from contemporary varnishes. They are made from natural resins such as copal and damar. Damar resin is relatively easy to use. Place lumps of damar resin and an equivalent amount of turpentine in a glass jar and seal securely. The jar should be shaken daily, and, over a number of days, the resin will eventually dissolve. It may need straining. Old varnish recipes used combinations of resins as each imparted particular properties to the final product. One might be used for its strength and another for its elasticity.

The natural color of varnishes varies greatly, as can be seen on the wooden panel opposite. The dark-colored shellac contrasts sharply with the yellow of linseed oil and the transparency of the modern acrylic varnish. Varnishes can also be colored with pigments. The pigments may have to be ground as otherwise they will appear gritty when the varnish is brushed out. Artist's oil paint can also be used for coloring oil-based or polyurethane varnish. The varnish must be stirred to ensure that the color does not sink to the bottom. Many classic varnishes included some form of coloring, such as dragon's blood or saffron which were used to simulate red and yellow mahogany respectively. One such recipe is as follows: *1 part gum benjamin, 2 parts Venice turpentine, 2 parts shellac, 4 parts sandarac.* Leave in a warm place until the gums are dissolved. Add denatured alcohol/methylated spirits until the mixture has the required consistency. Saffron can be added for color. Strain before use.

Varnishing must be done in a dust-free environment. It is usual to keep a special brush solely for varnishing. Use long, even brush strokes and apply the varnish as thinly as possible. Never overwork varnish as otherwise the brush strokes become visible and the surface will have to be sanded down. It is better to apply two or three thin coats rather than one thick one.

Varnished floors
Both the strong star-like design (above) and the tile-inspired pattern (right) have been created by the artist Thomas Lane, using varnishes colored with oil paints and pigments. The transparent property of varnishes allows the natural grain of the wood to show through, particularly with the lighter shades, and gives both floors a light and airy quality.

Shellacked furniture
This cabinet (above) has had layer after layer of shellac rubbed into it with a pad of cotton, until a high-gloss finish has been created. This highly skilled technique, sometimes known as French polishing, produces a very delicate finish.

Furniture varnishes
The wooden panel (left) has been painted and then had five different varnishes applied. From left to right these are natural linseed oil varnish, acrylic varnish, sandarac, polyurethane varnish, and a dark-colored shellac.

Liming

LIMING IS A traditional and classic finish. Every year, farmhouse walls were treated with lime-wash and then the remaining mixture was diluted and used on the woodwork. Wet lime is caustic, so it had the advantage of protecting the houses from bugs and bacteria.

Liming wax is a product made of white pigment mixed with beeswax that was used on floors in the 18th century. It can easily be made at home by adding white pigment powder to clear wax. It is more robust than traditional limewash, but it produces the effect of limed wood with a soft sheen. It gives a whitened or bleached effect which allows the grain of the wood to show through. Its very soft, subtle finish can transform heavy, dark, old-fashioned pieces into light contemporary furniture. The protective wax polish has a wonderful aroma which pervades the whole room.

The subtle effect of liming wax
This 1930s chest of drawers (right) was a gloomy piece of furniture in its original varnished state. By stripping it down and liming it, the oak grain is shown to its best advantage.

Liming wax on different woods
Oak (bottom) and pitch pine (below) are the most usual woods to be limed; they have a wide grain which takes the liming wax well. The wood can be stained with a dark color before lim-ing, or a black wax can be used in the grain to contrast with the pale wood.

Pitch pine

Oak

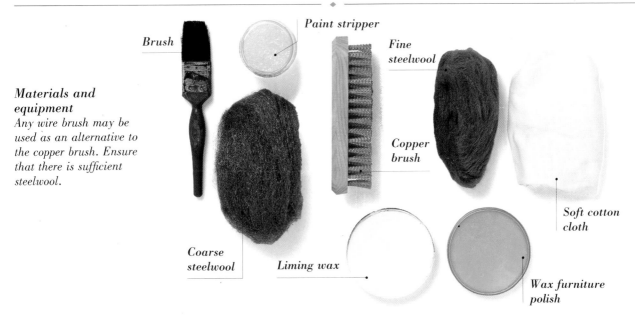

Materials and equipment
Any wire brush may be used as an alternative to the copper brush. Ensure that there is sufficient steelwool.

Brush

Paint stripper

Fine steelwool

Copper brush

Soft cotton cloth

Coarse steelwool

Liming wax

Wax furniture polish

LIMING A CHEST OF DRAWERS

1 Strip the wood and, if necessary, sand the surface until smooth. Push a wire brush in the direction of the grain to remove the soft wood.

2 Dip a piece of fine steelwool into the liming wax. Rub the wax into the wood, applying it both with and against the grain over the entire surface.

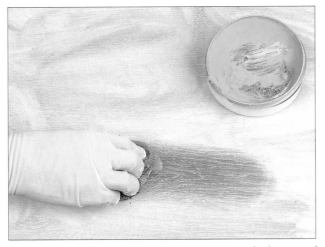

3 Leave it to dry for about 30 minutes. Dip a fresh piece of steelwool into wax furniture polish and rub it over the surface to remove the liming wax.

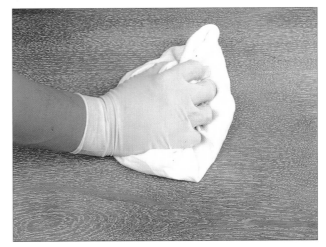

4 Buff up the surface with a soft cotton cloth. This gives a very soft, lustrous sheen to the finish, which may be rewaxed with clear wax from time to time.

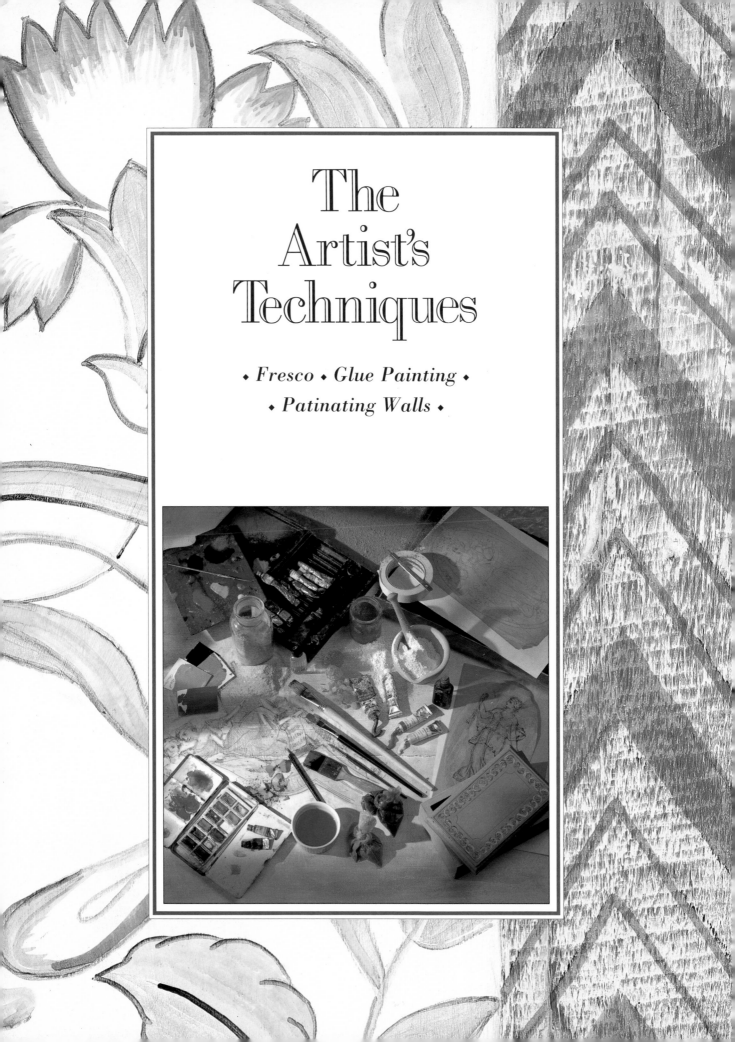

The Artist's Techniques

♦ Fresco ♦ Glue Painting ♦
♦ Patinating Walls ♦

HISTORICALLY, the skills and techniques of the decorative artist can be divided into two main categories: that of the highly-skilled, professional artist and that of the untrained painter, who might have been an itinerant craftsman or a farmer decorating his own home.

Professional work originated with Greek and Roman murals and developed during the Italian Renaissance, when the fine artist was initially apprenticed to a master. On completion of his apprenticeship, he was commissioned by leading Italian nobility and churchmen to decorate the walls and ceilings in grand villas, *palazzi*, and churches. These magnificent wall decorations were painted by men whose names are already familiar to us through their great works of art – for example, Giotto, Piero della Francesca, and Michelangelo.

At more or less the same period, a much simpler type of decoration was being painted on the walls of houses in Northern Europe. Unfortunately, few of these paintings have survived. Those that have range from quite simple designs to grander themes based on mythological, biblical, and classical characters. They were painted on walls, the backs of fireplaces, beams, and paneling. The colors that have survived are usually black, white, red, and Yellow Ocher; other colors may have been used, but have since faded or deteriorated. There was a vogue for blackwork embroidery which was then interpreted by painters as stylized geometric designs in black and

A detail of a fresco wall painting (left) by Fleur Kelly, shows the unique quality of this technique. The pigments are like a stain, allowing the texture of the plaster to show through.

white. Beams were often decorated with chevrons or elaborate zigzags. Painted cloths, imitating tapestries, were also hung on walls; these were as much for decoration as they were for warmth.

In England, following the civil war in the 17th century, skilled craftsmen were in short supply, as the puritanical Commonwealth regarded decoration as frivolous and ungodly. When King Charles II returned from exile, he looked to Flanders, France, Holland, and Italy for talented workmen. Antonio Verrio, for example, went to Britain at the King's behest to paint the walls of the palace at Hampton Court. These imported skills were based on the great tradition of fine art which had flourished in Europe and which can still be seen in the extensive painted work on walls and ceilings in great palaces and grand houses throughout the Continent. This type of work would often include *trompe l'oeil* – two-dimensional painting that deceives the eye into perceiving a three-dimensional scene – and *grisaille* panels and niches – monochrome painting simulating architectural details.

At a different level, decorative painting was popular all over North America and Europe. By and large, this work was carried out by untutored hands and has a directness and naïvety that is very appealing. Traveling painters would decorate the walls of the best rooms in a house for a small payment and their board and lodging. The subject chosen by early American settlers was often an idealized, Arcadian landscape; they also used stencils to make pretty designs and borders.

The types of paint used for wall painting varied as much as the character, technique,

Egg tempera, used on this frame (left), has long been a favorite for painted furniture, particularly in Scandinavia where the egg and pigment mixture was sometimes mixed with linseed oil. It dries to a very robust finish, which then toughens over the years, belying its soft, delicate, and flat/mat look.

Using the right brush for the job (right) makes it easier to work and can help to give the painting expression and make it livelier.

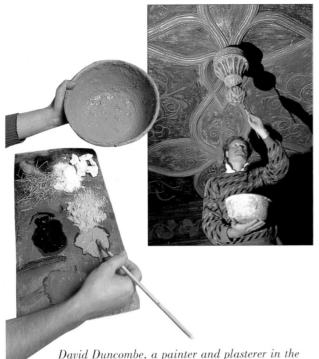

down and pigment added; when dry, it could be buffed to a light sheen. Egg tempera was not only used for frescoes but also for simpler decorative painting, particularly in rural areas. In Sweden it was a popular choice for painted walls and furniture. Milk in conjunction with lime was also used, particularly in America, and there is also evidence that pigment was mixed with rum and water, perhaps making some sort of spirit stain for plaster. Colored limewash was popular, especially for exterior work, in parts of Europe, such as Germany, Austria, and Switzerland.

Artists have always been patronized by the rich and so have traditionally been associated with high-quality work. The invention of mass-produced, cheap printed wallpaper in the 1830s brought about a decline in the patronage extended to decorative artists. Nevertheless, some work continued to be commissioned by the rich and there has been something of a revival in recent years. Many painters today were originally trained as fine artists and are now employed to make innovative and individual patinated walls and to research and use the materials of the past.

David Duncombe, a painter and plasterer in the medieval tradition, is shown at work on a ceiling (above). The lime plaster, made with horsehair and straw, was given a final smooth layer of plaster of Paris before the application of hand-molded plaster designs. Color was then applied and the work distressed by rubbing Raw Umber pigment over all the surfaces with a cloth soaked in a mixture of linseed oil, turpentine, and sand to make a fine abrasive.

You may feel reluctant to paint with the freehand techniques of the artist because of a lack of training. Many people think that they must be able to draw. While it is important to assess the weight and balance of a design, being able to draw is not necessarily a prerequisite. You can use source books, copy designs (which can be geometric), and plan your work on a smaller scale before you tackle a whole wall. Start with small areas, such as borders and friezes, to build up your confidence.

and themes across historical periods and geographical locations. Architectural conservationists and chemists have researched these, but some types have been more extensively documented than others. Italian frescoes used pigments painted into fresh lime plaster, for example. The paints for domestic and vernacular decoration were much more variable, depending on the availability of materials and local knowledge.

A mixture of pigments and animal glue was used for medieval paintwork. Also, wax was melted

Pen and ink work was popular for decorating pieces such as boxes (right) in the 18th and 19th centuries. Designs were usually drawn in black ink over white paint and then varnished. Classic Indian or Chinese inks can be used. Equally, as shown here, gouache or acrylics, thinned sufficiently to flow through a dipping pen, can work well.

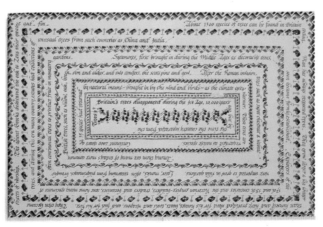

To transfer a design drawn on paper (above) onto a wall, the outline of the drawing is first pierced with a pin. A muslin pounce bag, filled with a dark pigment, is then rubbed over the paper, and the dotted outline of the image appears on the wall.

Fresco

FRESCO IS AN ancient, classic method of wall painting; some early examples are Greek, Etruscan, and Roman murals, and the frescoes of the Italian Renaissance. Fresco has an intrinsic beauty in the depth and subtlety of the colors. In *buon fresco*, the classic technique, pigments mixed with water are painted onto a surface of wet lime plaster; the lime acts as a binding agent and permanence is achieved when the lime chemically reacts to become calcium carbonate. It is a very long-lasting form of wall decoration as the pigment becomes part of the substrate.

Before painting a fresco, the wall surface must be carefully prepared. First it is plastered with a rough coat known as *arriccio*. Then a thin skin or *intonacco* is applied to the wall, and each day's painting must be completed before this dries. This is not so daunting as it sounds, since small areas can be mixed at a time, and dried plaster surfaces can be cut away at the end of the day. This is not difficult because the plaster remains fairly soft.

Inspiration can be found in classical sources, such as the temples of ancient Greece, the palace of Knossos, Roman villas in both Italy and other parts of Europe, the murals of Pompeii, and the wonderful paintings of Italian Renaissance artists such as Giotto and Michelangelo.

The example shown here is a whole room, which is a daunting task for anyone to undertake. We suggest that you might insert a small area into a wall; a permanent picture within the wall's surface.

The preparation of lime plaster must be carefully done; it is built up from a rough coat of lime putty and coarse sand. In addition to *buon fresco*, which must be done onto wet or fresh lime mortar,

Ageless beauty
This close-up of the wall (above) shows the textural beauty of the plaster surface and the softness of the color.

painting may be done onto partially dry mortar (known as *mezzo fresco*), or onto a dry lime mortar (known as *secco*). In the case of *secco*, a medium must be added to the pigment in order to bind it. This is usually egg tempera (*see page 131*), but can also be casein paint made from fresh skim milk and lime water (that is, the clear water that rises from lime putty when it is allowed to stand). Only lime-resistant pigments can be used in fresco, as lime is alkaline and would destroy acid-based pigments. (*See page 129 for a list of lime-resistant pigments suitable for use.*)

Fresco room
The fresco room (below and inset) was painted by Fleur Kelly. It was first mapped out and drawn to scale on the plan (left). The room serves as a small dining room and is simply furnished; the beauty of the fresco speaks for itself.

Some pigments are more suited to *buon fresco*. The traditional Italian fresco palette is white, black, red oxides, green and yellow earths, and Egyptian Blue, today replaced by Ultramarine.

It is possible to copy fresco technique by painting over rough or smooth plaster with white latex/vinyl emulsion and then painting over this base with acrylic paints. This can be rubbed back with the finest grade of sandpaper and then waxed with a hard wax, such as microcrystalline.

If the idea of painting a fresco seems overwhelming, a similar effect can be achieved by adding pigment to the plaster before putting it on the wall. By using large uneven amounts of pigment, a mottled effect can be created. Alternatively the pigment can be mixed in to achieve a solid, even color. This method is used in Italy, Spain, Portugal, and North Africa.

Preparing the surface
Here (below) are both sides of a section of wall made of lath and the first layer of lime mortar, known as arriccio, *which is a coarse mixture. The lime mortar is made up of lime putty and sand in a ratio of 1 part lime mortar to 3 parts sand.*

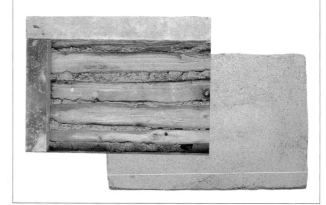

FRESCO TECHNIQUE

1 The final layer of mortar is a mixture of equal parts of fine sand and lime putty. This layer should be as thin as $\frac{1}{8}$ inch/3 mm thick.

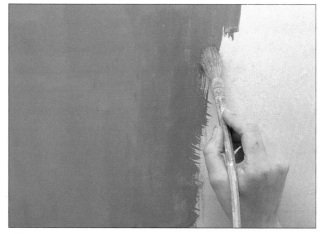

2 After leaving the wet intonacco *(thin skin) for 3–4 hours, start stroking and working up the pigments. It is important to get rid of the brush strokes.*

3 The details can now be added. Painting is done alla prima *(mistakes cannot be corrected) so it is important to work out the design in advance.*

4 This is a simple fresh design; more intricate paintings must be drawn in outline first and the outline transferred onto the wall.

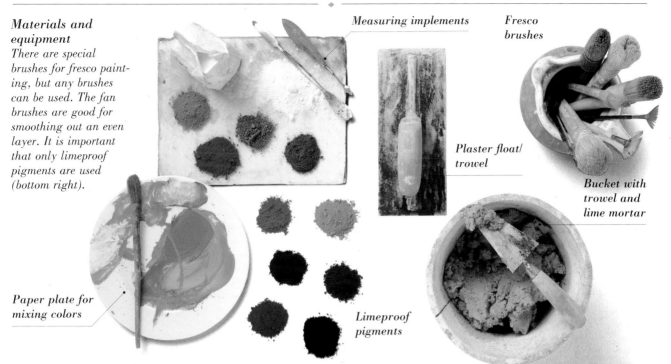

Materials and equipment

There are special brushes for fresco painting, but any brushes can be used. The fan brushes are good for smoothing out an even layer. It is important that only limeproof pigments are used (bottom right).

Measuring implements

Fresco brushes

Plaster float/ trowel

Bucket with trowel and lime mortar

Paper plate for mixing colors

Limeproof pigments

Buon fresco

Here (left) only a few colors are used, based on the Roman palette. This fresco technique is known as buon fresco – painting in pigment alone on fresh lime mortar.

Limeproof pigments

Ivory Black
Yellow Ocher
Mars Yellow
Naples Yellow
Siennas
Umbers
Cerulean Blue
Cobalt Blue
Ultramarine
Mars Violet
Red Oxide
Viridian
Oxide of Chromium
Green Earth

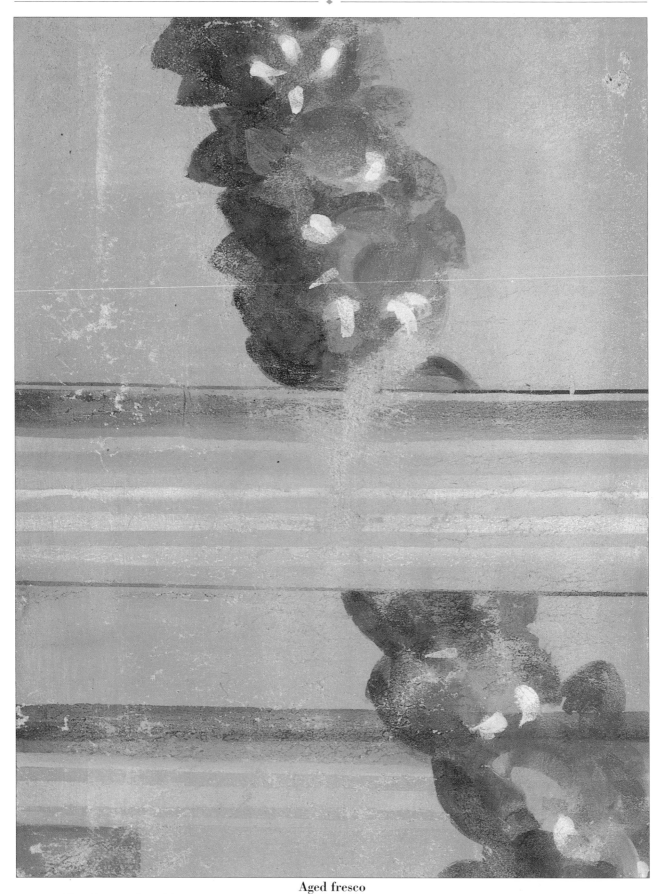

Aged fresco
This Romano-British buon fresco has been copied by Fleur Kelly from a section of the London Wall, now in the Museum of London. The distressed effect has been achieved by rubbing it back in places with sandpaper.

Tempera

When the lime plaster is dry, additional work can be carried out using tempera paint. Pigments are mixed with egg yolk, which binds the color together. It has a very beautiful finish; almost flat with a very slight sheen. It has a mellow, warm look. The yellowness of the egg yolk does not affect the colors.

Tempera was among the earliest paint used by artists. It is hard, durable, and almost waterproof. Paint made with egg tempera has proved to be more permanent than oil paint. The viscosity of the mixture can be altered by adding more or less water to it. Egg tempera has to be made up fresh and should really be used on the day it is made.

Oil of cloves or spike lavender

Ultramarine pigment

Egg yolk

Bowl

Knife

Spoon

Materials and equipment
All of these are very easy to obtain. The egg yolk sac can be either discarded or retained.

MAKING TEMPERA

1 Separate the egg and pierce the sac that holds the egg yolk. Allow the egg yolk to run into a bowl.

2 Add cold water and blend. The quantity depends on the thickness or thinness of paint required.

3 Add pigment to the paint and stir to ensure it is thoroughly mixed.

4 A few drops of oil of cloves or spike lavender may be added to prevent the paint from going moldy.

131

Glue Painting

P EOPLE HAVE used paint as a means of decoration since ancient times, and different types of paint have slowly developed and been improved, as research and technology has provided us with increasing information and materials. However, these new materials are not always so good for either the environment or the surface being coated as classic, natural-based paints.

One of the oldest forms of paint which is simple, safe, and easy to make, is so-called glue paint. It has also sometimes been known as size paint (*see pages 78–81*), although unlike most size paints such as calcimine/distemper, it was only made in small quantities for decorative work. Glue paint has been used since medieval times to decorate walls, wooden beams, and furniture. It is a common modern fallacy that houses in the Middle Ages had white walls and exposed darkened beams. In fact, most houses and their lime plaster walls were covered with a variety of designs and motifs.

Glue paint's continuing popularity over the following centuries owed much to the inexpensiveness and availability of its ingredients. In remote areas of Northern Europe, particularly Scandinavia, Germany, and Austria, the supply of milk and eggs for casein paint and tempera were often scarce in the winter months and glue would have been the obvious alternative.

Glue paint uses size to bind the pigment together and water as a thinner. There was no particular recipe – craftsmen had their own recipes, ingredients, and mixes. The size used as the base for glue paint was almost pure gelatine. It was made from whatever materials were readily available and therefore, the type of glue used varied from region to region. In the West, glues made from the skin, bones, and hoofs of animals were more common, while in other countries such as Japan, fish glue was the norm. The culture of the time dictated that nothing should be wasted and elsewhere allied forms of glue paint were developed, using flour made from wheat or rye, or sometimes even potato as a substitute for glue. A more complex form of flour paint is Finnish cooked paint (*see page 20*).

Today the glues most commonly used are calfskin glue or rabbitskin glue, which are sold in

Medieval decoration
This medieval decoration (right) was painted by the artist David Cutmore in a house in Sussex, England. The design for the strapwork and figures on the wall was taken from an original wall-painting dating from about 1550, which still survives in a house nearby. The design for the ceiling came from another local house, while the chevron patterns on the beams were common in medieval times and are thought to have symbolized generosity or gratitude. In attempting to get as close a likeness to the authentic colors as possible, the artist has used glue size paint colored with earth pigments.

Materials and equipment
These are the materials for both making glue paint and painting the design (see pages 134–135).

Various sable brushes

Spoons

Terre Verte

Venetian Red

Charcoal for drawing designs on the wall

Heatproof bowl for soaking rabbitskin granules

Yellow Ocher

Vine Black

Bain marie or double boiler

Vinegar

Rabbitskin granules

MAKING GLUE PAINT

1 Soak the glue overnight, using 1 part size to 10 parts cold water. The next day add a further 10 parts water to the size.

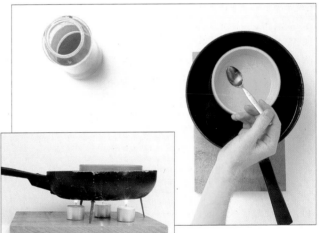

2 Add a few drops of vinegar to help prevent mold growth. Warm the granules gently with the water until they melt.

3 Put some pigment (here, Venetian Red) into a bowl and add a small amount of water to disperse it.

4 Add the size mixture to the pigment and stir until it is evenly mixed in. Use a hand-sized bowl.

granules or sheets. Calfskin glue is the cheaper option, but it is not so easily available and is less flexible, so it tends to be used for making larger quantities of paints, such as when making calcimine/distemper to cover a wall. Ideally the granules or sheets of size should be soaked overnight so that they fatten up. When the resulting mixture is heated, the granules melt and a slightly sticky liquid is formed. It reverts to a gel on cooling, but can be reheated to restore it to liquid form. You can test whether the paint has been mixed to the correct proportions by poking your finger into it when it has set. It should be the consistency of trembling jelly and fall away easily. If you need to apply some pressure in order to break it up then the mixture is too thick.

When making your own size, a few drops of vinegar should be added to help prevent mold growth as size goes bad after about ten days. It can be kept in the refrigerator, but it tends to thicken. If water is added to thin it, the glue becomes too dilute and the mixture is weak.

Medieval painters used terracotta paint pots the size of their hands. The warmth created from holding the pots kept the paint from solidifying. In order to melt the granules, David Cutmore, the artist at work here, has made a *bain marie* or double boiler, using a block of wood, some nails, a frying-pan, and some night lights. This allows him to work on site without having to return to the kitchen to reheat the rabbitskin granules. An ordinary heatproof bowl set over a pan of hot water will keep the paint warm and so prevent it from solidifying for quite a long time.

The pigments used here must be compatible with lime as they are applied over lime plaster. The wall painting David Cutmore demonstrates uses four colors – Venetian Red, Yellow Ocher, and Terre Verte, which are all earth pigments, and Vine Black, which was made by calcinating the young shoots of certain wood and other products.

Glue paint can be applied over lime plaster which has been given a coat of calcimine/distemper (whiting and glue size).

Unlike with fresco, where all painting is done *alla prima* (mistakes cannot be corrected), glue paint dissolves in hot water and so errors can be washed off.

PAINTING THE DESIGN

1 Make a freehand drawing of the design in charcoal. Use references if necessary.

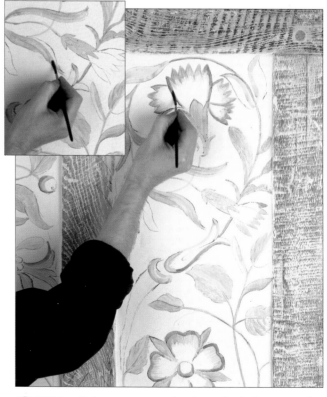

2 Fill in all the areas using the first color before proceeding to the next. Here, a long-haired lining brush or rigger is used.

3 *The dark lines are added to give strength to the overall design. The brush allows a flowing line and holds more paint than a short-haired brush.*

4 *The chevron was a popular motif on beams, which were painted to conceal the wood. The flat chisel brush allows thin and thick lines to be painted.*

5 *When the overall design is finished, the surface is distressed by sanding with fine wet and dry sandpaper. In this instance, it is used dry.*

6 *Burnt Umber is applied with a dry brush to rub back the colors and dull their freshness. Finally the pigment is pushed into the surface of the wall with fine sandpaper.*

Patinating Walls

IMEWASH, FRESCO, and calcimine/distemper mellow and develop with age in a particularly attractive way. Artists and decorators use a combination of techniques to imitate this patination. No special equipment is required – just a good eye for balance and tone.

Paint, depending on its type, age, and location, patinates in different ways. In tropical areas, it is often bright to begin with, but will fade and peel in the sun to reveal another color. It will not have the dirty layers of a wall in a smoky, northern city. For the effects of a dirtied wall, many artists will paint the first layer quite brightly, and then tone the color down in subsequent layers. If the colors are dull and muted from the start, the finished effect may look flat and lifeless. A little of the original bright

color should peek through the darker layers. The darker, dirty layer can be done in various ways. Raw Umber is the usual pigment used, but it can be applied in combination with other colors. The pigment is put in a medium, such as a glaze or a thinned mat varnish, and brushed and wiped with a cloth over the work. Sometimes dry pigment is rubbed over the slightly damp work.

When this layer is dry, sandpaper, steelwool, or sand and oil on a cotton cloth can be used to rub or scratch it away slightly to reveal the paint underneath or even the plaster or wooden base.

For a clean-looking patina, dry pigment is added to a wet wall and brushed out to give bright shocks of intense color. Other coats can be "frottaged." A second color is painted over a dry base color. Before it is dry, newspaper or plain absorbent paper is laid over the paint, rubbed, and quickly lifted off, thus removing the paint unevenly. Free-hand painting, stencils, and ragging or bronze powders can be incorporated to suggest old wall paintings which have been overpainted. To achieve the mat, dry texture of old walls, a mat varnish may be applied.

An old damask effect
This interior (left) is by the artist Geoffrey Lamb. The stenciled wall has been painted directly onto the plaster, but the basecoat had been distressed before the stenciling was applied.

A stone wall effect
Also by Geoffrey Lamb (above), the trompe l'oeil stone effect has been painted so that the colors and tones are variegated and uneven. It shows the importance of under-stating color and using a limited range of tones.

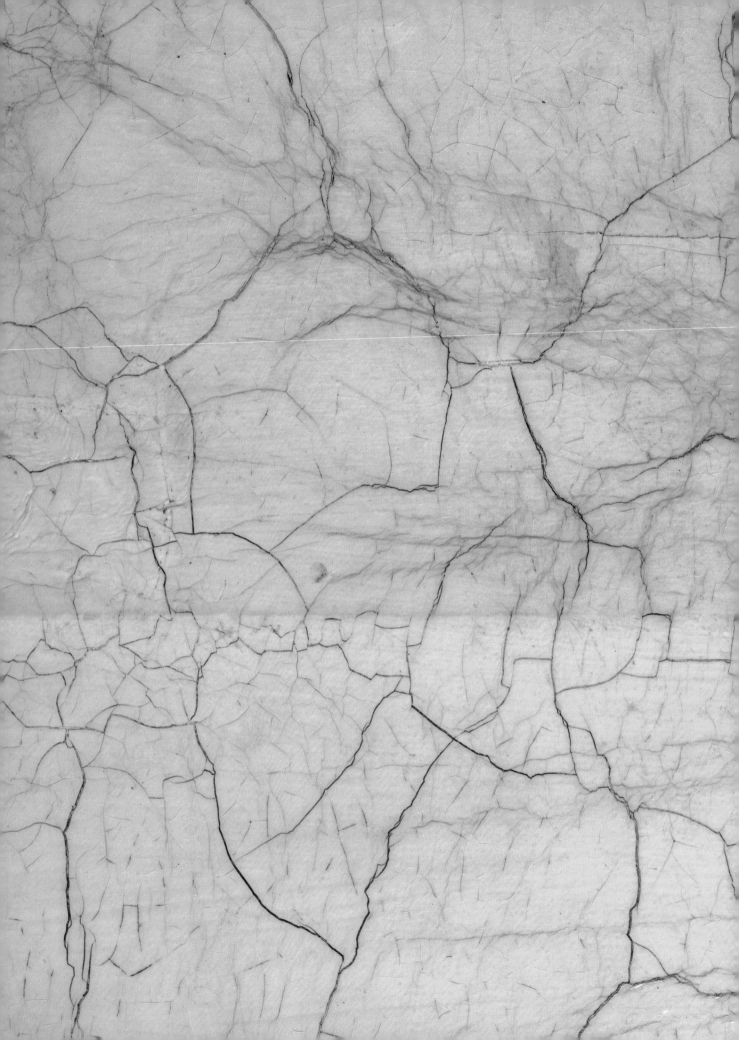

The Restorer's Techniques

♦ *Antiquing and Distressing* ♦
♦ *Crackle Varnish* ♦ *Peeling Paint* ♦
♦ *Verdigris* ♦

THE RESTORER'S TECHNIQUES described here simulate the character of antique furniture. Much of the beauty of antiques lies in the patina acquired over the years. Successive layers of wax bring out the color and quality of wood, while spots of oil, cracked varnish, dirt, small stains, scratches, and nicks all contribute to the character of a piece. A surface should have texture with a sense of history. Unfortunately, many pieces of painted furniture will have lost their unique qualities as a result of the vogue for stripped pine. Pine furniture was precisely the sort that would have been painted because pine was a cheap wood.

Regardless of the craftsman's original intention, most people want to see their antiques and fine art with layers of age and patina. In fact, many people are surprised and shocked at the clarity of color in a newly restored painting which they have been accustomed to seeing through accumulated layers of varnish and grime. You have to decide whether you want a piece of furniture to look as though it is antique, or whether you want it to appear as it was originally when the craftsman had just finished painting it.

Originally, furniture made from wood was left in its natural state, but in the 17th century, when the idea of designing a room as an integrated interior began to form, furniture was painted as part of the decoration. Relatively little of this old, painted furniture has survived in its original state as the current vogue for mellow, old paintwork is very much a 20th-century one. In the past, as soon as a piece was worn, it was repainted, regilded, relacquered, or "restored" in some other way. The pieces which have survived are now mainly in museums or grand houses, although examples can be found in some of the poorer communities, where "restoration" was too expensive an option.

Well-restored and painted pieces may look completely authentic. Unscrupulous dealers may pass off painted reproduction pieces as the real thing. Good, contemporary decorative artists do, of course, also use the techniques of the restorer simply for effect, with no intention of fooling anyone. In these cases, the modern provenance of the piece is usually indicated by a stamp or a mark.

A number of techniques can be used to imitate the character of old, worn, and repainted surfaces, some of which are described and illustrated in this chapter. They are simple techniques mostly involving the application of varnishes with different drying times, sanding back layers of paint, and applying and using paint in different ways. The skill lies in the application of the paint, varnishes, and waxes used and in the sensitivity with which colors are chosen. It is the feel and the character of the paint surface which is important.

To get you started, it may be valuable to look at reference books or to visit museums to get into the spirit. For example, if you are going to apply a crackleglaze, it may be better to brush it on in patches rather than all over the surface. Part of the

Plain clear waxes can easily be colored with dry powder pigments to achieve an exact color for matching purposes. When they are dry and set, the piece can be rubbed with sandpaper or steel-wool to give a good patina (above).

attraction of old-style furniture is the uneven quality of the finish. It should be darker in some parts, perhaps near the hinges or in corners, to suggest a build-up of wax and dirt. It should be worn and smooth in others, such as at the edges or around the handles, to suggest a well-used piece.

A knowledge of colors and of mixing colors is useful. Modern colors, particularly those made by commercial manufacturers, do not necessarily have the right "flavor" for decorating an old piece. They are often clean and bright and may need darkening by adding Raw Umber pigment, for example. Alternatively, the

This crackled mirror frame (left) has been aged by unevenly rubbing a cold, dark-colored wax over white paint applied over a red earth color. To achieve the deep cracks, a thick layer of crackleglaze was applied followed by a thick layer of white paint, both applied horizontally.

entire piece may be waxed with a dark-colored wax. Reproduction colors are a good choice or you may mix your own paints. Bright lemon yellows and bright red were not easily obtainable colors in past centuries, especially in the tougher oil paints which would have been used for furniture. Paint

Paintwork that will later be waxed with dark colors needs to be quite strongly colored if it is not to be obliterated at the waxing stage. In this sample (left), various colors have been painted over an ocher background. It is worth testing various samples before attempting a large piece.

palettes were restricted mainly to earth colors, some blues, and greens. Only the best pieces of furniture in grand houses may have used brighter, more expensive pigments.

It is not advisable to try out any of these techniques on high-quality, antique furniture. Restoring valuable antiques is a highly specialized skill which should be left to professional restorers. There are manufacturers of excellent reproduction furniture who will sell unpainted pieces for the decorative artist to work with; many of them copy Shaker designs. Good junk shops and markets are also invaluable sources.

There are well-tried techniques for distressing surfaces both before and after they are painted. These include hitting table tops with bunches of keys and other hard objects to make dents to suggest a worn surface. Some restorers also use a small drill to create holes to simulate woodworm infestation, and flick or spatter small dots of paint

onto the surface to suggest fly spots. (These same techniques can be applied using modern colors, without any allusion to time and antiquity, to create a stunning modern and elegant design.) Waxes can be colored with pigment, and crackle varnish and crackleglaze can be used in sharply contrasting colors. A surface may be dramatically changed through the use of different colors, varnishes, and waxes. It may be valuable to make a test sheet to try

The crackleglaze has been sandwiched between two very similar shades of off-white (left). After the last layer had dried, classical motifs were painted over. The motifs also peeled like old paint, even without a second layer of crackleglaze. It is best to draw motifs in pencil first. The mid-gray can then be painted, followed by highlights and other shades of gray.

out different ideas before time, money, and materials are wasted on expensive mistakes.

It should also be mentioned that these techniques and ideas need not be limited to furniture and other smaller pieces. They can be applied to walls, doors, and woodwork throughout the room to give character and a sense of time to an interior. The techniques, obviously, have to be employed on a larger scale, but since you will be dealing mostly with flat areas, there is no reason why they should not be undertaken.

An old door in France (left) has worn away around the keyhole through constant use. To achieve an aged look on furniture, think about where it would be most worn – areas such as corners, edges, handles, and drawers.

Antiquing and Distressing

THE WORDS "aged" or "antiqued" are used to describe a look rather than a specific technique, particularly on painted furniture, where the paint has darkened, worn away, and cracked over the years. There is a wide range of materials and techniques which can be used to achieve this look.

The simplest method is to paint a topcoat over the first basecoat and, when it is dry, rub down the paint surface with fine sandpaper, going through to the basecoat in some places and through to the wood in others. Those areas which are least worn will retain traces of the topcoat. The final stage is to rub the piece all over with furniture wax, making sure that all areas, cracks, and nicks have been covered. Buff to a sheen with a soft cotton cloth. The waxing process can be repeated to increase protection and luster.

Crackle varnish and crackleglaze may be used in a few areas and, in the case of crackleglaze, Raw Umber pigment can be rubbed into the peeled paint effect before it is varnished. Colors such as Raw Umber can be added to varnish but this may be tricky to mix. A ready-prepared antiquing or patinating varnish is available from art stores. After a final varnish has been applied, it can be rubbed back in places with coarse steelwool and the resulting scratches filled with "dirt," using a small amount of artist's oil paint on a small cloth. Some furniture is also distressed with deliberately inflicted dents and knocks. Fly spots and wood-worm holes can be fabricated by flicking a surface with dark paint. With all these techniques, the trick is to apply them unevenly.

Colors should be carefully considered too. Two colors are normally used, a basecoat and a second coat. The choice is obviously important; dark green on red and blue on orange simulate an old wood with a dark color on top, evoking old Irish or early American furniture. By using wilder colors, such as bright pink and lime green, with lightly colored wax over it, an effect reminiscent of Mexican, Caribbean, or Indian styles can be achieved. Colors that are close to each other in tone will give a soft, mellow effect. The idea is to expose the bottom layer of paint in areas where a piece of furniture would receive the most wear. Whatever colors are chosen, it should be remembered that they will be darkened by rubbing in the wax.

Peeled paint and sandpaper
Parts of this table (below) were crackleglazed over a dark green basecoat. The design, painted with an off white and a pale green, was rubbed back with sandpaper and varnished.

Wax and sandpaper

The basecoat of this small panel (right) was painted in a brown-red, water-based paint. When dry, this was given an uneven coat of green and a stencil was applied using a cream colored acrylic paint. This was alternately rubbed with steelwool and waxed.

Bedside cabinet
The top of a waxed and distressed bedside cabinet with rubbed back stencil and paint is shown (right). The base color may be rubbed down until smooth or deliberately left with brush marks, as here, so that the ridges of paint hold onto the wax.

STENCILING AND DISTRESSING A CABINET

1 *Two colors of acrylic paint, a light green and a clear blue, are mixed together thoroughly in a paint tray. Excess paint is worked off the brush.*

2 *A stencil is accurately positioned and the acrylic paint is carefully rubbed through.*

3 *The stencil design is repeated to form a border around the edge of the cabinet.*

4 *Clear wax and Ultramarine pigment are mixed together with a spatula until the pigment is thoroughly dispersed.*

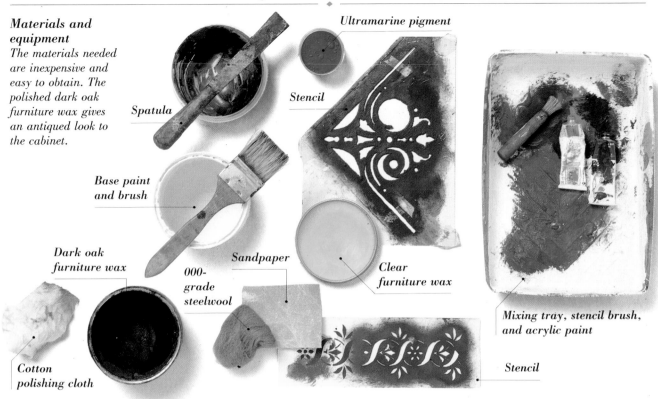

Materials and equipment
The materials needed are inexpensive and easy to obtain. The polished dark oak furniture wax gives an antiqued look to the cabinet.

Spatula

Ultramarine pigment

Stencil

Base paint and brush

Dark oak furniture wax

000-grade steelwool

Sandpaper

Clear furniture wax

Cotton polishing cloth

Mixing tray, stencil brush, and acrylic paint

Stencil

5 When the stencil is dry, the wax mixture is applied and rubbed into the surface with 000-grade steelwool.

6 The pigment–wax mixture is left to harden for 30 minutes before the surface is polished with a cotton polishing cloth.

7 A fine grade of sandpaper is used to distress the surface at random and to rub paint and wax off the edges.

8 Dark oak wax is rubbed on and polished over the surface with a cotton cloth to age and darken the colors.

Crackle Varnish

Decorators have always known that different materials may interact and cause surface cracking. Many old painting manuals describe how to avoid this, but here, this property is deliberately used as part of the technique. The finished effect is of cracked or crazed varnish, and it can be used over plain paint, découpage, stenciling, and freehand painting. It is not just an antiquing technique; over a deep red artist's oil paint, with gilt cream rubbed into the cracks, the overall effect can be stunning.

Crackle varnish, also known as craquelure, is sold in a package including two varnishes: one oil-based and the other a fast-drying, water-based product. The oil-based varnish is applied first and the water-based varnish is applied over it. An oil varnish with gum arabic over it may be used as a substitute. The difference in drying times produces hair-like cracks into which oil paint is rubbed to make them more visible. The longer the delay before the second coat is applied, the smaller the cracks will be.

Mock 19th-century table
This table (opposite) was given an off-white basecoat. After the crackle varnish was applied, Raw Umber and Ivory Black artist's oil paint were rubbed into the cracks to create an effect reminiscent of old ivory. A polyurethane varnish was applied to protect the finished surface.

Materials and equipment
The materials and technique required for a crackle varnish finish are simple. You may wish to experiment with drying times to determine the extent of the cracks. A little heat from a hairdrier helps to create the cracks. Too much will make the whole layer peel off.

Slow-drying oil varnish

Polyurethane varnish

Artist's oil color

Quick-drying water-based varnish

Cotton cloth

Brush for applying varnish

HOW TO APPLY CRACKLE VARNISH

1 *Apply a thin coat of the oil-based varnish over a clean nonporous surface with a soft brush. Ensure that it is evenly applied so that drying rates are the same. Allow to dry until it is slightly tacky.*

2 *Brush a coat of water-based varnish over the first coat while it is still tacky. Allow to dry for about 30 minutes, until cracks appear over the surface.*

3 *When the second coat is completely dry, rub a small amount of oil paint into the cracks with a cotton cloth. Wipe off the paint residue.*

4 *When it is dry, the surface must be protected with polyurethane varnish. The water-based varnish used for the crackle technique can be easily damaged.*

Peeling Paint

THIS TECHNIQUE, also called crackleglaze, simulates the appearance of old paint that has peeled and cracked to reveal a layer of paint underneath. It is very quick and simple to execute. Crackleglaze medium is painted between two coats of water-based paint. There are many commercial crackleglazes available. They are slightly different, but all work on the principle of a layer "sandwiched" between two paint surfaces. If a design is painted or stenciled over the second coat of latex/vinyl emulsion, it will also crack.

The type of water-based paint used is crucial. Some latex/vinyl emulsions have too much plastic in them; the crackleglaze needs to adhere to the paint rather than lie on it. It is always wise to test the underside of an object if you are not sure.

Gum arabic, available as a liquid or as crystals which dissolve in boiling water, may also be used. Two coats of gum arabic should be applied. When it is thoroughly dry, apply the second coat of latex/vinyl emulsion.

The effect of peeling can be reminiscent of exterior walls and woodwork, particularly when strongly different colors and tones are used. But if a more delicate and classical look is required, two similar colors, such as stone and a cream, should be used.

Materials and equipment
Make a test to ensure that the latex/vinyl emulsion will work. Reproduction 18th-century paints were used here. Aging varnish or a dark wax could be used as an alternative to polyurethane.

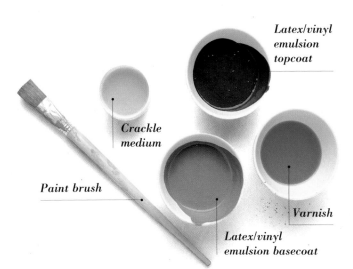

Latex/vinyl emulsion topcoat

Crackle medium

Paint brush

Varnish

Latex/vinyl emulsion basecoat

PEELING A SHAKER BOX

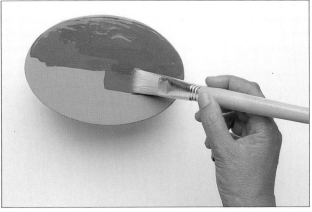

1 *Paint a coat of the base color and allow to dry completely. Using a suitable brush, apply the crackle medium either over the whole surface or just parts.*

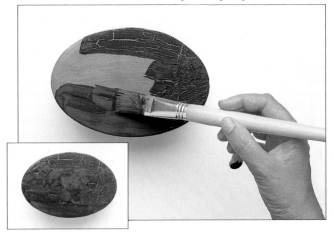

2 *When the crackle medium is completely dry, apply a second coat of paint in a different color. The crackle effect will start to take place almost immediately.*

3 *When dry, the surface can be given a coat of clear varnish for protection, or waxed with a dark-tinted wax, which gives an antiqued appearance.*

Peeled frame

To create these deep, wide cracks, this frame was painted twice with red gesso and, when dry, was covered with a thick layer of crackleglaze and allowed to dry overnight. A thick coat of white latex/vinyl emulsion was then painted over the dry crackleglaze. Finally, dark wax was rubbed in to create an aged look.

149

Verdigris

VERDIGRIS is the bluish green patina formed on copper, brass, and bronze by the corrosive action of air and seawater over time. It was also once used as a pigment, and was first discovered by the ancient Greeks. It had a beautiful, transparent color ranging from a pale green to a deep blue-green. It had to be isolated from other pigments by layers of varnish, as it was not compatible with many others. This color can be used to make a *faux verdigris* patina.

The pigment was originally made by putting copper or brass sheets into diluted acetic acid (vinegar). A green crust formed, which was used as a pigment. The pigment was not satisfactory, as it often turned black when exposed to air, and after the 19th century it was superseded by more reliable greens, such as Viridian. To make a verdigris patina, other copper-based green pigments or paints, such as Phthalocyanine Green and Viridian Green, can be used.

There are two basic methods for creating a verdigris patina: with paint or with chemicals on a copper leaf background. The first method is used for large areas, such as walls, plaster casts, and earthenware pots. Casein paint or any mat-textured paint is suitable, as these closely match true verdigris in texture. The technique involves three layers of paint. After the plaster has been sized (this stage is quite often omitted), it is first painted deep brown, Van Dyck Brown, for example. When dry, some areas are overpainted with a dark green glaze. Rather than using a brush, since brush marks are too recognizable, a rag or sponge may be used. The glaze should be made by mixing Phthalocyanine Green with a little white pigment, Titanium White for example, and some Raw Umber to give it depth. When this layer is dry, add another layer of the same color lightened with more white, applied with a stippling action. Decorative artists have developed their own individual methods of recreating the variations found in verdigris patination. On the wall opposite, for example, this metallic effect was created by using bronze powders.

The second method, for smaller areas, uses copper leaf which can be torn and stuck down. Household bleach is effective for corroding the metal to produce the desired patina.

Ancient lights
This wooden candlestick (below left) has been gilded with copper leaf. Household bleach has been flicked onto it to achieve a verdigris patina.

A sense of time
This personal and individual method was used by decorative artist Geoffrey Lamb in a London house (opposite). The look is inspired by old walls and antiquity, but has a fresh contemporary feel. This verdigris effect can be achieved by frottaging diluted latex/vinyl emulsion paints over a bronze powder and shellac background. Frottage is done by covering a freshly painted area with a sheet of paper or newspaper, rubbing it down, and then pulling it off to reveal a haphazard, uneven effect of color.

Suppliers

United States

H. Behlen & Bros., Inc.
4715 State Highway 30
Amsterdam, NY 12010
Tel: (518) 843-1380
Fax: (518) 842-3551
Resins, oils, gums, and waxes.

Benjamin Moore & Co.
51 Chestnut Bridge Road
Montvale, NJ 07645
Tel: (201) 573-9600
Fax: (201) 573-0046

Budeke's Paints
418 South Broadway
Baltimore, MD 21231–2486
Tel: (410) 732-4354
Fax: (410) 732-FAXX

**Charles Nevison
Architectural Accents**
2711 Piedmont Road
Atlanta, GA 30305
Tel: (404) 266-8700
Waxes and liming kits.

City Chemical
100 Hoboken Avenue
Jersey City, NJ 07310
Tel: 800-248-2436
Fax: (201) 653-4468
Resins, oils, gums, and waxes.

Cohasset Colonials
38 Parker Avenue
Cohasset, MA 02025
Tel: (617) 383-0110
Fax: (617) 383-9862

Constantine & Son, Inc.
2050 Eastchester Road
Bronx, NY 10461
Tel: (718) 792-1600
Fax: (718) 792-2110

Donald Kaufman Color
410 West 13th Street, 2nd floor
New York, NY 10014
Tel: (212) 243-2766
Fax: (212) 929-9816
*Acrylic paint and very finely
mixed paints.*

Hirshfield's Decorating Centers
725 Second Avenue North
Minneapolis, MN 55401
Tel: (612) 377-3910
Fax: (612) 377-2734

Janovic/Plaza, Inc.
30–35 Thomson Avenue
Long Island City, NY 11101
Tel: 800-772-4381
Fax: (718) 361-7288
*Catalog and mail order. Brushes,
paints, papers, and many
specialty items.*

The Johnson Paint Company
355 Newbury Street
Boston, MA 02115
Tel: (617) 536-4244
Fax: (617) 536-8832

Livos Plant Chemistry
1365 Rufina Circle
Santa Fe, NM 87501
Tel: (505) 438-3448
Fax: (505) 438-0199
*Natural paints and varnishes,
particularly for those sensitive to
normal paints.*

Loew-Cornell, Inc.
563 Chestnut Avenue
Teaneck, N.J. 07666
Tel: (201) 836-7070
Fax: (201) 836-8110
Natural and synthetic brushes.

**New England Resins and
Pigments Corporation**
316 New Boston Street
Woburn, MA 01801
Tel: (617) 935-8910
Fax: (617) 933-4417

**The Old Fashioned Milk
Paint Company**
436 Main Street
Groton, MA 01450–0222
P.O. Box 222
Groton, MA 01450
Tel: (508) 448-6336
Fax: (508) 448-2754
*Mail order. Traditional milk paint
with lime in powdered form, and
crackleglaze.*

O'Leary Paint
300 East Oakland Avenue
Lansing, MI 48906
Tel: (517) 487-2066
Fax: (517) 487-1680

PPG Industries, Inc.
1 PPG Place
Pittsburgh, PA 15272
Tel: (412) 434-3131

Purdy Corporation
13201 N. Lombard
Portland, OR 97203
Tel: (503) 286-8217
Fax: (503) 286-5336
Natural and synthetic brushes.

Sherwin Williams
101 Prospect
Cleveland, OH 44115
Tel: (216) 566-2000
Fax: (216) 566-3310

The Stulb Company
East Allen & North Graham Streets
P.O. Box 597
Allentown, PA 18105–0597
Tel: (215) 433-4273
Fax: (215) 433-6116
*Mail order. Reproduction paint
colours for the American Colonial,
Federal, and Victorian periods.*

Trend Lines
375 Beacham Street
Chelsea, MA 02150
Tel: (617) 884-8882
Fax: (617) 884-2485

Canada

Artist Emporium Ltd.
106–1135 64th Avenue S.E.
Calgary, Alberta T2H 2I7
Tel: (403) 255-2090
    800-661-8341
Fax: (403) 255-8780
    800-263-2329
*Oils, acrylics, pigments, dyes,
mediums, and woodstains.*

Barnes Artists Supply
132–10th Street N.W.
Calgary, Alberta T2N 1V3
Tel: (403) 283-2288
Oils, acrylics, and temperas.

Benjamin Moore & Co., Limited
139 Mulock Avenue
Toronto, Ontario M6N 1G9
Tel: (416) 766-1173
    800-387-8790 (Ontario)
Fax: (416) 766-9677
*Household paint, varnish, enamel
finishes, paint specialities, gold
and aluminium paint, paint
primers, and stains.*

Chateau Paint Inc.
440 Beaumont West
Montreal, Quebec H3N 1T7
Tel: (514) 495-1713
    800-361-4601 (for area codes
    514, 819, 418, 613)
Fax: (514) 271-1006
*Household paint, wood coatings,
decorative finishes, and varnish.*

Cloverdale Paint Inc.
6950 King George Highway
Surrey, British Columbia V3W 4Z1
Tel: (604) 596-6261
Fax: (604) 597-2677
*Household paint, varnish, stains,
coatings, and enamels.*

Crown Diamond Paints Ltd.
3435 Pitfield Boulevard
St-Laurent, Quebec H4S 1H7
Tel: (514) 332-3602
    800-363-0150 (Quebec,
    Atlantic Provinces)
Fax: (514) 745-4155
*Household paint, enamels,
finishes, varnish, shellacs,
and acrylics.*

EZ Paintr, Canada
1155 Barmac Drive
Weston, Ontario N9L 1X4
Tel: (416) 748-7229
Fax: (416) 748-9506
*Natural and synthetic brushes,
and rollers.*

Flecto Coatings Ltd.
1455 Lakeshore Road,
Suite 203 South
Burlington, Ontario L7S 2J1
Tel: (416) 333-6545
    800-663-1608 (British Columbia)
    800-361-0246 (Ontario)
    800-361-2152 (Quebec)
    800-361-2228 (Atlantic
    Provinces)
Fax: (416) 333-924
*Household paint, specialty paint,
"environmentally friendly"
specialty coatings, plastic and
synthetic enamels, thinners and
cleaners, synthetic resin finishes,
stains, and varnish.*

Gemst Inc.
5380 Sherbrooke West
Montreal, Quebec H4A 1V6
Tel: (514) 488-5104
Fax: (514) 488-9343
*Pigments, varnish, paint, wax,
temperas, oil paints, and
oil mediums.*

Glidden Paints
8200 Keele Street
Concord, Ontario L4K 2A5
Tel: (416) 669-1020
    800-387-3663
*No-solvent latex paints in three
finishes. Faux finish clinics.*

Interlab Paints, Inc.
490 Des Meurons Street
Winnipeg, Manitoba R2H 2P5
Tel: (204) 233-0800
    800-665-8889
Fax: (204) 237-5534
*Household paint, varnish, wood
finishing products, specialty
coating products, enamels, gold
and aluminum paint, rubber base
paint, paint primers,
preservatives, and stains.*

**International Paints
(Canada) Limited**
19500 Trans Canada Highway
Baie d'Urfe, Quebec H9X 3S8
Tel: (514) 457-4155
Fax: (514) 457-4108
*Trade paint, stains, wood finishes,
oils, and acrylics.*

LePage's Limited
50 West Drive
Brampton, Ontario L6T 2J4
Tel: (416) 459-1140
Fax: (416) 453-8671
Woodstains and finishes.

Maiwa Handprints
6–1666 Johnston Street
Granville Island, Vancouver
British Columbia V6H 3S2
Tel: (604) 669-3939
Fax: (604) 669-0609
*Acrylics, varnishes and mediums,
bronze powders, wood and fabric
dyes. Cutting tools, stencil
brushes, and sponges.*

A. R. Monteith (77) Limited
2615 Wharton Glen Avenue
Mississauga, Ontario L4X 2B1
Tel: (416) 270-0311
Fax: (416) 270-0160
*Customized coatings and
wood finishes.*

Niagara Paint & Chemical Co.
2 Hillyard Street,
Box 402, L.C.D. #1
Hamilton, Ontario L8L 7W4
Tel: (416) 522-4604
Fax: (416) 572-6177
*Household paint and finishes,
coatings, enamels, paint primers,
paint specialties, and shellac.*

Niagara Protective Coatings
7071 Oakwood Drive
Niagara Falls, Ontario
Tel: (416) 356-1581
Fax: (416) 354-2077
*Household paint, gold and
aluminum paint, plastic paint,
paint primers, resin emulsion
paint, rubber base paint, paint
specialties, acid- and alkali-
resisting varnish, and
wall coatings.*

L'Oiseau Blue Artisanat Inc.
141 Ste-Catherine East
Montreal, Quebec H1V 1X2
Tel: (514) 527-3456
Fax: (514) 527-6348
Oils and acrylics.

Omer DeSerres
334 Ste-Catherine East
Montreal, Quebec H2X 1L7
Tel: (514) 842-6637
    800-363-0318 (Quebec)
Fax: (514) 842-1413
*Oils, acrylics, alkyds, fabric paint,
stencils, brushes, and other fine
art material.*

Peinture UCP Paint Inc.
1785 Fortin Boulevard
Laval, Quebec H7S 1P1
Tel: (514) 381-9217
    800-361-9465
Fax: (514) 668-9553
*Decorative coatings, vinyl-based
coatings, enamels, lacquers,
finishes, and stains.*

Pittsburgh Paints
5546 Timberlea Boulevard
Mississauga, Ontario L4W 2T7
Tel: (416) 238-6441
    800-441-9695
Fax: (416) 238-6450
*Household paint, latex products,
odorless alkyds, acrylic latex,
linseed oil and other stains,
and varnish.*

Reid's Art Materials Ltd.
5847 Victoria Drive
Vancouver, British Columbia,
V5P 3W5
Tel: (604) 321-9615
Fax: (604) 324-REID
*Oils, acrylics, alkyds,
and brushes.*

Sheffield Bronze Inc.
710 Ormont Drive
Weston, Ontario M9L 2Y5
Tel: (416) 749-8800
   800-668-4808 (Ontario)
Fax: (416) 749-8659
*Bronze powders, decorative
enamel, metallic finishes, paint
colorants, tinting colors, paint
specialties, lacquers, brushes,
and rollers.*

Sherwin Williams Canada Inc.
170 Brunel Road
Mississauga, Ontario L4Z 1T5
Tel: (416) 507-0166
Fax: (416) 507-4198
*Household paint, paint in heritage
colors, varnish, stains, enamels,
lacquers, and special coatings.*

Sico Inc.
2502 De la Métropole
Longueil, Quebec J4G 1E5
Tel: (514) 527-5111
   800-463-SICO (General
   information, Quebec)
   800-361-6310 (Orders, across
   Canada)
Fax: (514) 646-7699
*Household paint, protective and
decorative organic coatings and
related products, varnish,
lacquers, primers, stains,
colorants, thinners, surface
conditioners, and preservatives.*

**Société Internationale Canadienne
Tobgi Inc.**
2301 Guénette Street
Montreal, Quebec H4R 2E9
Tel: (514) 745-1551
Fax: (514) 745-1552
*Acrylics, temperas, oil paint, and
designer gouache.*

**Stevenson DL & Son Artist's
Colour Mfg. Co. Ltd.**
1420 Warden Avenue
Scarborough, Ontario M1R 5A3
Tel: (416) 755-7795
Fax: (416) 755-5895
*Oil colors, acrylics, acrylic
mediums, oil mediums,
and brushes.*

Talens C.A.C. Inc.
2 Waterman Street
St-Lambert, Quebec J4P 1R8
Tel: (514) 672-9931
   800-361-2101
Fax: (514) 672-4754
*Paint, acrylics, oils, temperas,
and brushes.*

**Tower Paint, a Division of
Cloverdale Paint Inc.**
15846–111 Avenue
Edmonton, Alberta T5M 2R8
Tel: (403) 451-3830
   800-232-1911 (Alberta)
Fax: (403) 452-1601
*Household paint, plastic paint,
plastic coatings, finishes, synthetic
enamels, paint primers, paint
specialties, and varnish.*

United Kingdom and Ireland

Auro Ireland Ltd.
Doon Lough, Fivemilbourne
Sligo, Co Leitrim, Eire
Tel: (071) 43452
Natural paints and varnishes.

Auro Organic Paints
White Horse House, Ashdon
Nr. Saffron Walden, Essex
CB10 2ET
Tel: (0799) 584 888
Fax: (0799) 584 887
*Mail order. Full range of organic
paints, pigments, and varnishes.*

Biofa Natural Paints
5 School Road, Kidlington
Oxford OX5 2HB
Tel: (086 75) 4964
*Natural and environmentally
sound paints, pigments,
and varnishes.*

Brome & Schimmer Ltd.
3 Romsey Industrial Estates
Romsey, Hampshire SO51 OHR
Tel: (0794) 515595
Fax: (0794) 830370
*Mail order. A large range of plant
dyes, such as alkanet, logwood,
and fustic.*

H. J. Chard & Sons
Albert Road
Bristol BS2 0XS
Tel: (0272) 777681
Fax: (0272) 719802
*Mail order. Pigments and
materials for limewashing and
lime mortar.*

Cornelissen & Son Ltd.
105 Great Russell Street
London WC1B 3RY
Tel: (071) 636 1045
Fax: (071) 636 3655
*Mail order. Artist quality brushes,
pigments, gilding materials, resins,
gums, and paints.*

Craig and Rose plc
172 Leith Walk
Edinburgh EH6 5EB
Tel: (031) 554 1131
Fax: (031) 553 3250
Oil glazes and varnishes.

Cy-Près
14 Bells Close, Brigstock
Kettering , Northants NN14 3JG
Tel: (0536) 373431
*Specialist suppliers and
contractors for the maintenance of
historic buildings. Wide range of
materials including Stockholm tar,
lime mortar and putty, fresco
materials, oil colors, zinc oxide
paints, barn paints, pigments,
copperas washes, distempers,
and limewashes.*

Environmental Paints Ltd.
Unit 11, Dunscar Industrial Estate,
Blackburn Road
Egerton, Bolton BL7 9PQ
Tel: (0204) 596854
Fax: (0204) 309107
*Mail order. A range of decorative,
interior, solvent-free paints.*

Farrow & Ball Ltd.
33 Uddens Trading Estate
Wimborne, Dorset BH21 7NL
Tel: (0202) 876141
Fax: (0202) 873793
*Mail order. Specialist and
traditional paint manufacturers,
who produce the National Trust
range of paints, in oil undercoat,
dead flat oil, oil eggshell, oil full
gloss, estate emulsion, oil bound
distemper, and soft distemper.*

Foxwell and James
57 Farringdon Road
London EC1M 3JH
Tel: (071) 405 0152
Fax: (071) 405 3631
*Mail order. Restoration products
including waxes, shellacs, and
gold paints.*

Heart of the Country
Home Farm, Swinfen
Nr. Lichfield, Staffordshire
WS14 9QR
Tel: (0543) 481612
Fax: (0543) 481684
*Mail order. American
reproduction colors.*

Hirst Conservation Materials Ltd.
Laughton, Sleaford
Lincolnshire NG34 0HE
Tel: (0529) 7517
Fax: (0529) 7518
Traditional and historical materials such as lead paints, limewashes, lime mortar, lime putty, soft and oil bound distemper, milk paint, and pigments.

Liberon Waxes Ltd.
Mountfield Industrial Estate
Learoyd Road, New Romney, Kent
TN28 8XU
Tel: (0679) 67555
Fax: (0679) 67575
Mail order. A wide range of wood-finishing and restoration products.

Livos Paints
P.O. Box 103
Warwick CV34 6QZ
Tel: (0926) 400821
Fax: (0926) 400821
Mail order, with a three day delivery service. A range of exterior and interior household paints and varnishes, which are made from plant and mineral extracts, and are particularly suitable for those sensitive to normal paints.

E. Milners Decorators' Merchant
Glanville Road, Cowley
Oxford OX4 2DB
Tel: (0865) 718171
Fax: (0865) 770942
13 Lombard Street, Abingdon
Tel: (0235) 521131
Large range of specialist painters' and decorators' materials.

John Myland Ltd.
80 Norwood High Street
London SE27 9NW
Tel: (081) 670 9161
Fax: (081) 761 5700
Mail order. Many traditional materials such as stains, polishes and shellacs, waxes, pigments, pearl glue, rabbitskin glue, varnish brushes, and lining brushes.

Nutshell Natural Paints
10 High Street, Totnes
Devon TQ9 5RY
Tel: (0803) 867770
Newtake Cottage, Staverton
Devon TQ9 6PE (Mail order)
Tel: (0803) 762329 (Mail order)
Range of products based on natural materials including emulsion paints, casein paint in powdered form, earth and mineral pigments, varnishes, oils, waxes, stains, and citrus peel oil solvent.

John Oliver Paints
33 Pembridge Road
London W11 3HG
Tel: (071) 221 6466
Specialist paints, with a range of deep colors, and a range of historic colors.

Papers & Paints
4 Park Walk
London SW10 0AD
Tel: (071) 352 8626
Fax: (071) 352 1017
Mail order. Large range of specialist paints, including two reproduction historic ranges. Materials for decorating furniture and interiors, including brushes, glazes, pigments, and varnishes.

Picreator Enterprises Ltd.
44 Park View Gardens
London NW4 2PN
Tel: (081) 202 8972
Fax: (081) 202 3435
Materials for professional restoration and conservation, including Renaissance wax polish.

Pine Brush Products
Stockingate, Coton Clanfield
Stafford ST18 9PB
Tel: (0785) 282799
Colourman reproduction paints and specialist brushes.

E. Plotons Ltd.
273 Archway Road
London N6 5AA
Tel: (081) 348 0315
Fax: (081) 348 3414
Mail order (SAE for catalogue). Glazes, artist's colors, stenciling and gilding materials and equipment, and specialist brushes.

Potmolen Paint
27 Woodcock Industrial Estate
Warminster, Wiltshire BA12 9DX
Tel: (0985) 213960
Fax: (0985) 213931
Mail order. Traditional paints including several types of distemper.

Putnams
34 Somali Road
London NW2 3RL
Tel: (071) 431 2935
Fax: (071) 794 2586
Mail order. Range of bright colors using pigments from the Mediterranean area.

J. H. Ratcliffe
135a Linaker Street
Southport PR8 5DF
Tel: (0704) 537999
Oil glazes, decorative glazing materials, tools, and brushes.

Relics
35 Bridge Street, Witney
Oxon OX8 6DA
Tel: (0993) 704611
Fax: (0993) 704611
Mail order. Colourman reproduction paints, the Liberon range, waxes, oil glazes, shellacs, and stencils.

Rhodes Design
86 Stoke Newington Church Street
London N16 0AP
Tel: (071) 275 8261
Fax: (071) 275 8262
Furniture for painting based on the Shaker style.

St Blaise Ltd.
Westhill Barn, Evershot
Dorset DT2 0LD
Tel: (0935) 83662
Fax: (0935) 83017
Mail order. Traditional paint, lime mortar, lime putty, soft and oil bound distemper, and limewash.

Sawyers Farm Ltd.
Little Cornard, Sudbury
Suffolk CO10 0NY
Tel: (0787) 228498
Fax: (0787) 227258
Mail order for seeds. Dye plants, such as indigo and madder. (Nursery only open on Saturdays.)

The Shaker Shop
25 Harcourt Street
London W1H 1DT
Tel: (071) 724 7672
Fax: (071) 724 6640
Mail Order. American reproduction paint and painted and unpainted Shaker furniture.

Stuart R. Stevenson
68 Clerkenwell Road
London EC1M 5QA
Tel: (071) 253 1693
Fax: (071) 490 0451
Mail order. All gilding materials, pigments, resins, gums, and artist's materials.

A.F. Suter
Swan Wharf, 60 Dace Road
London E3 2NQ
Tel: (081) 986 8218
Fax: (081) 985 0747
*Mail order. A wide range of
natural gums, waxes, and resins.*

**Whistler Brushes (Lewis Ward
& Co.)**
128 Fortune Green Road
London NW6 1DN
Tel: (071) 794 3130
*Extensive range of innovative
specialist brushes. UK distributors
of the famous 'Omega' range of
varnish brushes.*

Australia

Anne Lockyer Design
27 The Parade
Norwood, SA 5067
Tel: (08) 362 4722

Bristol Decorator Centre
76 Oatley Court
Belconnen, ACT 2617
Tel: (06) 253 2404

Carey Martin
190 Latrobe Terrace
Paddington, Qld 4064
Tel: (07) 368 3067

The Complete Look
20 Karalta Road
Erina, NSW 2250
Tel: (043) 652 922

Contrast Colour
79 Darley Street
Mona Vale, NSW 2103
Tel: (02) 979 5698
Fax: (02) 979 6695

Handworks
121 Commercial Road
Prahan, Vic 3181
Tel: (03) 820 8399

Harper & Sandilands
9 Almeida Crescent
South Yarra, Vic 3141
Tel: (03) 826 3611

Hornsby Paint Warehouse
89 Hunter Street
Hornsby, NSW 2077
Tel: (02) 477 7122

Janet's Art Supplies
143–145 Victoria Avenue
Chatswood, NSW 2067
Tel: (02) 417 8572
Fax: (02) 417 7617

Kayedar Pty Ltd.
89 Tennant Street
Fyshwick, ACT 2609
Tel: (06) 280 6673

Manfax Hardware
166 Gertrude Street
Fitzroy, Vic 3065
Tel: (03) 419 4166

Marsden Bros.
9 Chesterman Street
Moonah, Tas 7009
Tel: (002) 723 088

Middle Head Hardware
928 Military Road
Mosman, NSW 2088
Tel: (02) 960 1518

Natural Home Centre
P.O. Box 1344
Bowral, NSW 2576
Tel: (048) 621 818

Old Style Interiors
55 Bailey Street
Adamstown, NSW 2289
Tel: (049) 562 878

Oxford Arts Supplies Pty Ltd.
221–223 Oxford Street
Darlinhurst, NSW 2010
Tel: (02) 360 4066
Fax: (02) 360 3461

Paddington Fiveways Hardware
241 Glenmore Road
Paddington, NSW 2021
Tel: (02) 361 6928

The Painted Earth
6 Leura Street
Nedlands, WA 6009
Tel: (09) 389 8450
Fax: (09) 386 6351

The Painted Finish
4th Floor, 15–19 Boundary Street
Rushcutters Bay, NSW 2011
Tel: (02) 360 2795
Fax: (02) 331 7941

Paint Traders
228 Scarborough Beach Road
Mount Hawthorn, WA 6016
Tel: (09) 444 5744
Fax: (09) 444 2443

**Peter Sudich Discount
Art Supplies**
155 Katoomba Street
Katoomba, NSW 2780
Tel: (047) 82 2866
Fax: (047) 82 1318

Porter's Paints
11 Albion Way
Surry Hills, NSW 2010
Tel: (02) 281 2413
Fax: (02) 281 5724

Porter's Paints
592 Willoughby Road
Willoughby, NSW 2062
Tel: (02) 958 0753

Randwick Art and Craft Supplies
203 Avoca Street
Randwick, NSW 2031
Tel: (02) 398 3375

**Shoalhaven Recycled
Building Centre**
290 Princes Highway
Nowra, NSW 2541
Tel: (044) 232 324
Fax: (044) 233 456

S.A. Surface Coatings
2/61 O'Sullivan Beach Road
Lonsdale, SA 5160
Tel: (08) 326 4144

The Stencil House
662 Glenferrie Road
Hawthorn, Vic 3122
Tel: (03) 818 0421

Style Finnish
164 Arthur Street
New Farm, Qld 4005
Tel: (07) 358 3300

New Zealand

Country Colours
10 Broadway
New Market, NZ
Tel: (0011 64) 3 65 8234

Mcleister Painted Finish Products
Box 1669 GPO
Christchurch NZ
Tel: (0011 64) 3 65 6167

Index

Credits and Acknowledgments

Working on this book has been a tremendously challenging and rewarding experience. It has led to us meeting an enormous number of people whose knowledge, advice, and encouragement have been invaluable. In particular, we would like to thank the professional artists and decorators whose specialist expertise we relied on in certain sections of the book. These are:

Serena Chaplin (**Gesso** and **Lacquer**), who runs gilding and lacquer courses. *32 Elsynge Road, London, SW18. Tel: 081 870 9455.*

David Cutmore (**Glue Painting**), who is an artist in the medieval tradition on walls and wall hangings. *River Hole Cottage, Partridge Lane, Wadhurst, East Sussex, TNS 6LB. Tel: 0892 782543.*

Tennille Dix-Amzallag (**Oilgilding** and **Découpage**), who does decorative gilding and découpage on small items. *21 Gilston Road, London, SW10. Tel: 071 351 0059.*

Peter Hood (**Size Paints** and **Simple Oil Paint**), who is a consultant and surveyor-designer for ancient buildings and historic materials. *Old Lodge, Brigstock Parks, Northants, NN14 3NA. Tel: 0536 373439.*

Fleur Kelly (**Fresco**), who is a painter in fresco and egg tempera. *33 Northampton Street, Bath, BA1 2SW. Tel: 0225 330002.*

Thomas Lane (**Woodstains**), who paints, stains, and varnishes floors as well as doing other interior work. *57 Wellington Row, London E2 7BB. Tel: 071 729 6195.*

François Lavenir (**Bronze Powders** and **Lining**), who is a professional decorative artist. *13 Crescent Place, London, SW3. Tel: 071 581 1083.*

Andrew Townsend (**Limewash**), who is an architectural conservationist. *Marlborough House, 2 Bromsgrove, Faringdon, Oxon, SN7 7JG. Tel: 0367 242639.*

Very special thanks are due to Cornelissens, Linova Natural Paints, Patrick Baty of Paper and Paints Ltd, and Stuart Stevenson, for their amazing generosity in providing advice and materials.

We would also like to thank Margaret Balardie for her enthusiastic and invaluable advice on lacquer, Sally Hughes for the stunning calligraphic painting on the mirror and drawing board, Jane Steele for the delightful tray she decorated, and Joanna Walker for taking time out of her busy schedule to paint the inspirational green sun table.

In addition, we are also most grateful to Countess Monika Apponyi, Margaret Bradham, and Margaret and Andrew Townsend, all of whom allowed us to photograph in their homes, and to Auro Paints, Brome and Schimmer, Joris Arts of Patino, Livos Paints, Milners Paints, John Myland Ltd, Putnams Mediterranean Paints, and Whistler Brushes (Lewis Ward and Co.), who were all also very generous in providing us with materials.

Many others gave up their time to help us, including the Bevans, Eri Heilijgers, Geoffrey Lamb, Annie le Painter, Val Maclay, Patricia Monahan, Graham Moss, Maggie Philo, and Ellen Young.

As always, a book such as this one is created by a team, and a great deal of thanks is due to Geoff Dann for his superb photography and Steven Wooster for his sensitive and creative design. Most of all we would like to give very heartfelt thanks to Linda Doeser for keeping a tight rein on our unruly text and being so patient and cheerful with us. Lastly, we are very grateful to Colin Ziegler for his enthusiasm and hard work when our energies were flagging.

With the exception of those listed below, all the photographs in this book were specially taken by Geoff Dann for Collins & Brown Limited.

Architectural Association/Richard Glover: 48 bottom left, bottom center, and bottom right. Bolton Museum and Art Gallery: 83. Christie's Images: 111. Edifice/Darley: 48 top, 50 bottom left, 53 top. Edifice/Jackson: 60 bottom right. Edifice/Lewis: 19 top right, 50 top, 51 top left. Edifice/Ryle-Hodges: 110. Ian Howes: 39 bottom left, 51 top right, 53 bottom. Zara Huddleston: 38 top, 49 top and bottom, 52 bottom, 141 bottom left. Fleur Kelly: 124 top right. Thomas Lane: 118 bottom right and bottom left. Livos: 15 top left. Zul Mukhida: 52 top. Uulatuote Oy: 50 bottom right. Ian Parry/Traditional Homes: 132. Sikkens Paint Museum: 2, 14 bottom, 60 top right. John Ferro Sims: 51 bottom. Rob van Maanen: 61 bottom left. Ruud Velthuis Reklame: 60 top right. Elizabeth Whiting and Associates: 119 top. Jerry Williams/Traditional Homes: 125 top and top left.